Talking about Prayer

Talking about Prayer

RICHARD BEWES

Christian Focus

Christian Focus Publications publishes biblically-accurate books for adults and children. The books in the adult range are published in three imprints.

Christian Heritage contains classic writings from the past.

Christian Focus contains popular works including biographies, commentaries, doctrine, and Christian living.

Mentor focuses on books written at a level suitable for Bible College and seminary students, pastors, and others; the imprint includes commentaries, doctrinal studies, examination of current issues, and church history.

For a free catalogue of all our titles, please write to
Christian Focus Publications,
Geanies House, Fearn,
Ross-shire, IV20 1TW, Great Britain

For details of our titles visit us on our web site
http://www.christianfocus.com

ISBN 1 85792 613 7

Published in 2000 by
Christian Focus Publications,
Geanies House, Fearn, Ross-shire,
IV20 1TW, Great Britain

Cover design by Owen Daily

Contents

Part 1: THE LIFE OF PRAYER

Part 2: THE HEART OF PRAYER

Part 3: THE WORK OF PRAYER

FOREWORD

I hope this readable little book will find its way into the hands of Christian people on every continent, for it will have an immediate appeal to thousands who are rediscovering the life of prayer, both individually and through innumerable prayer groups that have mushroomed into existence everywhere in recent years.

Learn the secret of prayer! Through Christ we can find in God a heavenly Father, who hears and answers prayer. It is true to say that anyone who ever advanced as a Christian and whose life counted for the kingdom of God has been a person of prayer. It is my firm belief that *Talking About Prayer* could significantly strengthen the invisible network of praying people that God has brought into being around our world. God bless you as you read this book.

Billy Graham

INTRODUCTION:

AN AFRICAN AT AMSTERDAM

It was, perhaps, the most internationally representative gathering, political or religious, in all history – the Billy Graham Conference for preaching evangelists at Amsterdam. Certainly it put the United Nations in the shade. They had come from the greatest cities on earth, but they had also emerged from tropical forests, from the mountains of central Asia, from the African bush and the tundra of the Arctic – to pray and plan for the evangelisation of the world.

In the vast *Europa* hall, a sole African was kneeling in prayer on the concrete floor, oblivious of those criss-crossing the arena around him, as they busied themselves with the conference schedule. Nearby, Norman Sanders of the Billy Graham team was eyeing the prostrate African, concerned for his comfort. As he put it to me later, 'He'd been kneeling there for a long time'.

– 'And what might you have been supposed to do?' I asked.

– 'Well, I was Amsterdam's "Arrangements

Secretary"', said Norman.

– 'Arrangements, eh? Arranging what, Norman?'

– '*Everything*, man! It was my job to see that guys like that African evangelist knew of the amenities that I had arranged for their comfort! Only a few yards away there was a special prayer chapel that I had set up, with carpet, comfortable seats, soft drinks, everything. I didn't like to disturb our friend on the floor there, so I left him alone for a period, while I attended to another assignment. But when I returned to the *Europa* hall fifty minutes later, there he was, in the same place, still praying! I figured I might just let him know of the chapel nearby. First, I strolled over to the chapel to check that everything was all right. You know what I found in there? Four other delegates – all from the West. *And all four were fast asleep*!

It is an irony about the life of prayer, that the real work tends to get done in the unlikeliest of places. I knew a man called George Hoffman; he became one of the world's great humanitarian workers, and before his untimely death had been honoured by the Queen for his labours. He once told me that he became a follower of Christ when in the air force – but the prayer of decision was uttered on his knees in the camp toilet, because – as he put it – 'It was absolutely the only place where you could be assured of having some space genuinely to yourself.'

Prayer. I would never have chosen to write a book on the prayer life. What a subject – and how hypocritical one feels in making the attempt! This cannot be an exhaustive treatise; the very idea that anyone could cover the whole field of prayer in a kind of technical manual is ridiculous.

But there may be some simple guidelines in these pages, that can be put to use in our churches and fellowship groups. There is no vital need to read this book in a methodical, consecutive way. Although, for the sake of convenience, the chapters have been grouped into sections, I have deliberately tried to let each chapter stand on its own, so that the reader can feel easy about dipping into the pages at random.

Prayer is a lifelong education. It is caught as much as taught – as Norman Sanders and I learnt while we were at Amsterdam, from the focused prayers of a solitary African. Let's pursue this goal together.

Richard Bewes
London, England

Part 1

THE LIFE OF PRAYER

I would like to rise very high, Lord,
Above my city
Above the world
Above time.
I would like to purify my glance and
borrow your eyes.

Michael Quoist, Prayers of Life

The God of Israel, the Saviour, is sometimes a God that hides Himself but never a God that is absent; sometimes in the dark, but never at a distance – Matthew Henry

1

SEEING IN THE DARK

It was a cat. Or so I thought, as I stared through the twilight at the dark shape silhouetted on the grass. Softly I walked up the garden path. Yes, it must be a cat.

'Hullo, hullo, hullo – psst!' I hissed into the gloom. Not a movement. I stepped a little closer. Suddenly I realized that I was talking to a watering can.

On such occasions you quickly look right and left, in case anyone has witnessed your foolishness! Nobody likes being caught jabbering into thin air.

And really this is what, to some people, makes the age-old habit of prayer so incomprehensible. It is understandable that there are those who like holding one-way conversations, perhaps on the phone. I myself have been the receiver of such calls. A reassuring grunt or two from my end – that was all that seemed required. But for total silence to prevail in the face of persistent and repeated one-way conversations – wouldn't that indicate that the line was dead, or that the individual being called was simply not around? The absurdity of such an experience finds expression in the lines of Hughes Mearns:

As I was going up the stair
I met a man who wasn't there

Yet prayer has persisted, despite every discouragement, because it is principally an exercise of faith. Faith can be better understood when we think of its opposite. The opposite of faith is *sight*. If you could *see* the jet airliner from Tokyo as it approached London Heathrow where you were eagerly awaiting your friend, you would hardly need to pin your faith to the information being flashed to you at the arrivals desk. As it is, you accept what the airport authorities tell you, and confidently make your way – in faith – to meet your friend at the barrier. The information given you, backed by your past experience of airport efficiency, was enough. You had faith in British Airways.

Prayer is an exercise of faith in the invisible God. This faith is, as the New Testament puts it, 'to be certain of what we do not see' (Heb. 11:1). The quality of faith in a man like Moses is described graphically – 'as though he saw the invisible God' (Heb. 11:27). But it is never *blind faith.* Basically, faith is simply a response to a given set of factors.

True faith, far from being blind faith, is *informed faith.* I remember seeing a troupe of trapeze artistes in London. The climax of the act was to be a blindfolded leap by one of the girls, whose male partner was to catch her from the far side of the arena. The act required perfect timing, and the atmosphere became hushed and tense – only to be relieved by enthusiastic applause as the young woman successfully completed her leap. Faith? Yes, you could say that she had the faith to believe she would be safely caught – but you could never describe her act as a venture of *blind* faith, even though she was, in fact, blindfolded. There had been a wealth of training and experience to prepare her for the act, and, in addition, she had the shouted instructions of her partner to guide her as she made the leap.

God is invisible to us – and yet informed faith has a way of 'seeing' him nonetheless, as certain factors are weighed. We must face, for instance, the sheer impossibility of explaining the existence of a world populated by thinking, rational people, by saying that it sprang from an unthinking, meaningless existence. (Now that *is* blind faith!) Rational beings must have a rational origin.

True, the novice Christian has been persuaded by the evidence offered, that the universe is built on God's authority, and that this world is not left to itself. Now he is to prove this for himself, practically, in a daily experimental way. This happens in the life of prayer, as we learn to communicate with God and share every day with him. But how do we talk to God? And for how long? And with what phraseology?

Are there rules for the prayer life? Rules ... it's probably the wrong word for what is, after all, a relationship. What rule – or technique – was ever laid down for falling in love, or for strengthening the bonds of love? But there can always be guidelines. When operating a computer, I don't need a constructor's manual in order to get results, but it is a help to be told which controls to use. So with the life of prayer. God has given us his promises. Christ has given us a pattern, and steadily – sometimes stumblingly – we can learn to follow it, and progress is made. At certain times prayer seems arid and unproductive. I have noticed with young believers that a typical 'sticky' period occurs two years or so after the initial decision to follow Christ. But this is normal Christianity! It is easy enough to pray when life with Christ is novel, exciting and eventful.

But to persist in prayer when everything is flat – that indicates *real* progress. For by our persistence we are, in effect, saying, 'I know you are there, Lord, because I have your word for it. I know you are listening, because you say that you are. I know you have a plan for this world because of Christ – and by my prayer life I choose deliberately to involve myself in your plan for our world.'

Naturally there will be practical encouragements: occasions when the curtain is pulled back a little; God-given events, taking the form, often, of quite 'minor' happenings. If we have eyes to see them, they serve to confirm us in our basic belief that, yes, we are not on our own and the sky is not closed off!

I remember hearing of a speaking engagement involving a staff member of a major missionary enterprise in England. On his way to the meeting he realized, at the bus stop, that he was a penny short of his fare. He felt in his pockets with dismay. 'Never mind,' he reflected, 'we've been trusting God for thousands of pounds a year; why can't I trust him for a penny?' And leaning back against the bus stop shelter, he closed his eyes and prayed – for a penny. He felt a tap on his shoulder. A voice spoke in his ear. It was a friend: '*A penny for your thoughts*'! Naturally

19

enough the penny was claimed, and the prayer was answered!

Whether you yourself are going to be involved or not, *prayer is going on*. You can take a stroll round Red Square, or along Kenyatta Avenue, or up Princes Street, Edinburgh, and you can be certain of rubbing shoulders with men and women who pray. You could be watching the Chicago Bears or listening to the music in the Sydney Opera House, and quite certainly there will be people near you who believe in God and believe in prayer; who have been prodded by the available information into believing that this world is not left unattended, that the receiver is not off the hook – but that the lines are open, and that the God and Father of our Lord Jesus Christ is alive and in action!

The Lord lives!
Praise be to my Rock!
Exalted be God, the Rock,
My Saviour!

(A Prayer of David,
2 Samuel 22:47)

Prayer is the pulse of life – Andrew Murray

It is futile to pretend that prayer is indispensable to man. Today he gets along very well without it – Jacques Ellul

2

A LOST ART?

There is a town in the centre of Africa called Jinja. I have passed through it on more than one occasion. It is a significant place, and for one reason only – it straddles the very source of the Nile, where the waters of Lake Victoria have, for centuries, boiled out with unimaginable power into a narrow channel, only to cease flowing three and a half thousand miles later in the Mediterranean. These waters were harnessed in the mid-fifties when the prestigious Jinja Dam was completed, so providing Uganda with millions of kilowatts of generated electricity.

'Jinja to me is a parable,' said John Wilson, himself a product of Uganda, and a leading light in the work of *African Enterprise* before his untimely death in the 1980s. We were drinking tea just before John was to address a meeting. 'In Uganda's infancy,' he went on, 'we Africans regarded that place at Jinja with superstitious fear. It was a place to walk past quickly, a place to keep away from. But then,' and he smiled expansively, 'we found it to be a source of power. It provided for our lighting, our heating, our cooking and our industry. It took us a long time to realize the potential of that place!

'It is the same with the driving power behind Christianity,' continued John Wilson. 'All too easily we walk quickly past it, not realizing what it represents. Only in recent decades have we in Africa tasted the power of the Gospel and of living prayer. Meanwhile many of you in the West have largely forgotten it!'

If prayer has become a lost art in much of contemporary life, it is because of its apparent irrelevance in today's computerised, digital society. 'Ask, and you shall receive' are the words that take many back to their Sunday school days, but is there today a curiously redundant ring about them? We tend to be on the receiving end of plenty of this world's goods, even when prayer has gone out of the window, and deep down we know it. Indeed, people who never pray often appear better off materially than their more devout neighbours. One sympathizes with Christians praying for a spouse, when surrounding unbelievers appear to have no difficulty in acquiring partners.

But this is no new phenomenon. 'I had nearly lost my foothold,' confesses David the psalmist, centuries ago. 'For I envied the arrogant when I saw the prosperity of the wicked' (Ps. 73:2-3).

But what did we expect? That God would heap his gifts upon the believing world and keep the wicked short? If so, our expectations rise no higher than the standards set by the gods of Greek mythology. God – the only true God – is for the world! His gifts are given, irrespective of creed or obedience. The rain falls on the just and unjust alike. The harvests, our health – yes, and the phenomenon of love between the sexes – are part of the Creator's universal generosity, with no strings attached. Illogically, we have often imagined that personal discipleship carries with it the guarantee of special material benefits, and protection from accident and disease. If that were so, Christianity would be no more than a gigantic insurance policy.

As it is, we are confronted with reality when we read of the wicked that they are 'always carefree, they increase in wealth' (Ps. 73:12). The picture continues to look rosier for the unbeliever until, like the psalmist, we go 'into the Temple' and see, from within our life with God, the full story of unbelief from end to end. It is a tragically short story. It is a story of ephemeral one-dimensional people, living for a world of temporary benefits only – 'They are like a dream that goes away in the morning' (Ps. 73:20 RSV). How different from believers! Of them we read, 'You guide me with your counsel, and afterwards you will take me into glory. Whom have I in heaven but you?' (Ps. 73:24, 25).

What then is the point of prayer – for did not Christ promise, 'Ask, and you will receive'? Perhaps this promise is best interpreted in the light of our Lord's further promise, 'How much more will your Father in heaven give the Holy Spirit to those who ask him!' (Luke 11:13) Here are primarily *spiritual* blessings – available for redeemed, two-dimensional people, people of the Spirit, permanently and eternally secure.

Not that believers confine their prayers only to the field of the specifically 'spiritual.' Far from it. As we wake in the morning, the film of the day ahead begins to roll again before our minds: the encounters, the problems, the openings. Already, even before a verbal prayer has been composed, we are reaching out in spirit for the resources that will enable us for another episode in our stay on the planet Earth.

The tragedy of one-dimensional, materialistic people is not that they ignore this source of power, as the Ugandans of old hurried past the waters of Jinja. Rather it is that they never even realize that there is a potential for them to fulfil at all. John Henry Newman put it well:

Fear not that your life shall come to an end, but rather fear that it shall never have a beginning.

One of the great benefits of MILLENNIUM PRAYER becoming a world-wide hit was that a whole new generation of people learnt the Lord's Prayer for the first time in their lives – Sir Cliff Richard, 'Open Home, Open Bible' programme, February 2000

3

THE RIGHT NAME

It was a Friday evening when I got out at the station and made my way along Platform Four. It had been a 'broadcasting day' for me. I reached the station exit as the train pulled out once more.

Let me see now, I would be editing the programme tape this evening. Then I remembered. My briefcase – with the precious tape inside! At that moment it was recumbent in the rack just above my recently-vacated seat. By now it was irrevocably on its way to Southend. I quickly made for the little ticket office.

'Er, excuse me ... I left a briefcase on that train. Is it possible for me to get it back?'

The man behind the grille mechanically reached for a pad. 'Right, if you give me the details we'll get a form filled in and you –.'

'A form? But how long will it all take?'

'Oh, ten days. Maybe a week. What name?' The ball-point was already poised.

'Ten days! But' – and in desperation I

29

clawed at the one lever I had – 'there's a BBC tape in the briefcase. It's for a programme in two days' time.'

'The BBC?' Form and ball-point were forgotten as a hand stretched for the telephone. 'We'll get your case sent back on the next train from Southend, sir. It'll be about an hour.'

The BBC. Certain names seem invested with that extra touch of authority. You use the name and something stirs somewhere. Things get done. Even miracles take place!

When it comes to our dealings with God, however, there is only one name in the field. It is of little avail to plead in our prayers that we know the Reverend So-and-so at the local church and he will put in a word for us! For centuries, praying people have concluded their petitions with the words 'through Jesus Christ our Lord', 'for Jesus Christ's sake'. It is the one name we feel we have confidence in mentioning. Down the ages many prominent and holy people have been outstanding in their quest for goodness. But the further their progress, the greater was their awareness of their own need of forgiveness – of someone behind whose name they themselves could shelter in their approach to God. One man only was different. In the battle against sin and death, one man alone has done it!

Here is the historical basis of our Christian confidence in prayer. It is our belief that Christ has, by his saving death, dealt with the problem of our guilt, and secured a valid entry into God's presence for all who will acknowledge him as their now living mediator.

True, there are theologians today who question whether it *matters* that Christ historically died and rose again. They will argue that it is the meaning of the resurrection, as it affects our experience, that counts in the long run, regardless of whether or not the event took place at all.

But to say this is, as missionary strategist Colin Chapman states, reminiscent of the story *Alice in Wonderland*, where the *grin* of the Cheshire Cat survives even after the cat himself has disappeared!

'Well, I've often seen a cat without a grin,' thought Alice, 'but a grin without a cat! It's the most curious thing I ever saw in all my life.'

There's only one thing more curious, emphasizes Colin Chapman – a resurrection meaning without a resurrection event. No, these theologians themselves appear to be in a wonderland.

Millions of people take the Gospel accounts as authentic, and have accepted Christ as the unique, historical mediator, in whose authority they come to the Father in prayer. 'You may ask me for anything in my name,' he once declared, 'and I will do it' (John 14:14).

Lest any of our Lord's listeners imagined that his words virtually contained a magical blank cheque, available to all claimants, we have an amplification of them a little later, in the assertion: 'If you remain in me and my words remain in you, ask whatever you wish, and it will be given you' (John 15:7). About these words the great Bishop Ryle commented, 'He that would have answers to his prayers, must carefully remember Christ's directions.' But of course. The person who maintains a right relationship with Christ and, through study of his words develops an understanding of his purposes, will learn to ask for the right things. These requests will be granted.

Therefore God exalted him
to the highest place
and gave him the name
that is above every name,
that at the name of Jesus
every knee should bow,
in heaven and on earth
and under the earth,
and every tongue confess
that Jesus Christ is Lord,
to the glory of God the Father.

*(From the apostle Paul,
Philippians 2:9-11)*

What matters is the faith which lays hold on God and touches the heart of the Father who knew us long before we came to him – Dietrich Bonhoeffer

4

IN THE FAMILY

'Daddy, we want to camp tonight!'

I looked at our youngest two, both under ten years of age. It was Grandpa's garden in which they wanted to sleep out, for we were spending some days' holiday in Bexhill on Britain's south coast.

'Can we, Daddy? ... Daddy?'

Why not? Away they rushed to make their preparations. The organizing of the little tent. The sleeping bags. The torch, books and innumerable accessories so vital to the camping life. It is all very exciting when you have never done it before on your own.

It is perhaps not quite so *attractive* when the darkness falls and those strange night sounds begin. And you are out there on your own. Under ten years of age. The apprehensions had begun to be voiced earlier on. What will happen if it rains? Can bats get into a tent? Supposing a fox comes into the garden?

But I had thought of all that in advance. I'd studied the weather forecast in the paper – in fact I'd rung the Met. people for the latest details. I'd gone round the garden with a toothcomb, stopping up every crack and opening. I made the little tent as cosy and snug as I could. And then, as night began, I would steal out for a frequent peep at that vulnerable tent with its two sleeping occupants. It was impossible for me to go to bed myself. I couldn't help it. I would be standing, gazing out of the window into the garden. Then a cup of coffee. Minutes later would see me tip-toeing out again for another check. A listen at the tent entrance for the sound of breathing! And so the long night wore on.

So they had their apprehensions and concerns? They were nothing to mine! I was far ahead of them, anticipating, watching, protecting. After all, I was their dad.

Father ... 'This little word', writes Martin Luther, 'conceived effectually in the heart, passeth all the eloquence of Demosthenes, Cicero, and of the most eloquent rhetoricians that ever were in the world.' Luther was writing of the revelation of God's character as Father, which Jesus came to bring. The picture he gave us is unique.

The Muslims have some ninety-nine different names for God. Creator, Enricher, Watcher, Avenger – these different names will feature in a Muslim's prayers. Not one of them is 'Father'. But it would be impossible for a Christian to compile a list of even two or three names for God, without 'Father' being one of them. It is the name by which we know him best.

Jesus was responsible for that. True, the Old Testament pictures God as *Father* of Israel, of the nation. But it was Jesus who revealed a new intimacy about God's fatherhood. A privileged relationship of prayer was presented to his listeners – that of coming to one's own heavenly father. It is the relationship enjoyed by the three-year-old who doesn't wait to be asked, but jumps into bed for an early morning snuggle in the parental bed. In the mind of Jesus, this was *the* attribute about God, which from then on was going to give colour to all the rest.

The implications of this for the prayer life are enormous. The person who, through faith in Christ, has entered 'the family' of God, no longer regards prayer as a means of twisting the arm of a reluctant deity, of squeezing favours out of a distant and all-powerful benefactor. As one of the old Bible commentators puts it, 'What a distance between us in our helplessness and God in his glory, but "Father" reaches all the way!'

It was in the light of this relationship that Christ taught his hearers not to fret about their daily needs. 'Your heavenly Father knows that you need all these things,' he reassured them (Matt. 6:32). Certainly they were to ask for their daily bread – even if they knew it would be coming anyway. *This is how relationships are built*. The child asking for his pocket money on a Saturday morning is inwardly assured that he's not going to miss out on it. But he asks all the same – and meanwhile the family relationship is growing.

On a visit to Germany I met a seventeen-year-old African student in Grossalmerode. He had fled from his country under pressure from the military regime. His cousin had been murdered, and then his brother had been taken. On learning that he, too, was wanted, he disappeared over the border. 'I suffered a lot in Nairobi,' he told a group of us. 'I was terribly short of food and money. But Jesus had found me two years earlier in Africa, and so I prayed to my heavenly Father to guide me to those who could advise and help me. Now it has been made possible for me to come to Germany to complete my education. Although my family are far away, I am very thankful that I have a heavenly Father. I want now to sing you a song of praise!' And he did, without accompaniment, at the supper table.

None of us is without our fears and apprehensions. But those who have, through Christ, entered into a personal relationship with God, have made the discovery of someone they learn to call their 'Father'. Fears, hopes, joys and disappointments alike they learn to bring to him. Yes, and their grumbles and doubts. No matter if they have no polished phrases with which to approach him. He is, after all, their Father. And then, as they progress in their membership of his family, they learn with surprise that he is not without a measure of concern for their affairs. On the contrary, in his fatherly protection and watchfulness he is ahead of them. Far, far ahead of them!

A believer is surely a lover, yea of all lovers the most in love! – Soren Kierkegaard

5

WHAT DOES PRAYER DO?

'I do you good gully-gully!'

No one who has seen the gully-gully men of Port Said can ever forget them. An Arab in voluminous clothing would stand, surrounded by a circle of fascinated tourists. A live, fluffy, yellow chick would be held in the palm of a brown hand.

'One chick!'

The chick's head was then apparently broken off, and suddenly, 'Two chicks!'

The operation was then repeated.

'Four chicks!'

Before long it seemed as if the place was alive with fluffy, yellow chicks.

How was it done? It was certain that, in one way or another, those flowing voluminous clothes held a good many secrets!

How is it done? Does it work? What results can you get? It is natural for us to ask such questions when we come to the topic of prayer, and we sometimes look for the quick answer. But once we understand a little of what prayer is, we can see that we are asking the wrong questions. For prayer consists neither of magic to produce illusions, nor of a technique for obtaining results! Too often we have read the biographies of praying giants such as George Muller, whose orphanage work was supported through prayer to the tune of thousands of pounds. Then the subtle whisper intrudes itself upon our thinking, *God never does that for you, does he?*

For you? It is sheer arrogance to treat God as though he were the office boy, the errand-runner, fetching and carrying on our behalf. For the activity of true prayer places God unconditionally at the centre of the scene. Prayer is the vital means by which he has chosen to involve us in his actions, regardless of any sensational results that we may see. The test is whether we love him enough to maintain our prayer link with him, when the skies seem like brass and dramatic answers are as rare as the Koh-i-noor diamond.

Why pray at all, then? Because we *love* God, and want to keep in touch with him! Prayer is not given us so that we can make use of God for some purpose outside of himself. Do we *use* those whom we love? It is better, if we are to think of errand-boys at all, to see ourselves in the servant role, presenting ourselves in our prayer times before the God we have come to love. It's as though we say, 'Is there anything I can do for you?' For the astounding thing is that God has apparently chosen not to act without our co-operation. And prayer is his greatest chosen way of involving us in his actions. As Augustine of old put it, 'Without God we cannot; *without us he will not.'*

Look at it like this. There are certain people we love and admire – people for whom we will do virtually anything, however inconvenient. Indeed, far from 'an inconvenience', we count it an honour to serve their needs. A telephone call comes through:

> 'I wonder if I could have your help? I'd be so grateful if you would be kind enough to take the early morning train into town, meet my ageing mother at the coach station, give her some breakfast and see her safely onto the Heathrow Express, in time for her flight at 11.30.'

A privilege? Of course.

Such things we could not do easily for *everybody*. But for someone we admire and look up to above any others? For the God of all the universe? Prayer is really a test of our love of God. Is it not true that as our love for him grows, so we *want* to avail ourselves of the privilege, not only of communicating with him as our friend every day for friendship's sake, but of putting ourselves at his disposal and co-operating in his actions, for love's sake?

At times there may well be a lifting of a corner of the curtain, a hint, a loving indication that he took my prayers, yes even mine, and acted upon them in some distant place. Or even on the spot before my eyes! If so, that is all bonus.

I used to know a clergyman called Joe Coffee. One day, on his way to take a funeral, he walked into the local garage to pick up his car which had been in for servicing and was now ready for collection. But on that day there had been a muddle, and his car key had become mixed with some others. Now it was lost in a hopeless jumble, among a pile of miscellaneous car keys, scores of them together on a tray. 'We're very sorry,' Joe was told, 'but we think yours may be somewhere here.'

There was no time to be lost. Any delay would mean that he would be late for the funeral. Joe Coffee paused a second. Then, standing in front of the startled garage hands, he shut his eyes. 'Which one is it, Lord?' he asked aloud. Then he plunged his hand in among the tangle – and pulled out his own key!

He got into his car and drove off, leaving the garage hands looking at each other.

How was it done? No, it's futile to ask such a question. We're not in the business of multiplying chicks, or of pulling diamonds out of hats. *We're in the very life of God.* And when events such as Joe Coffee's take place – however rare they may be – they are worth far more than that bare supplying of a need. We find ourselves gasping, 'Why, God himself actually heard, he took notice of *my* praying!' God's world has been opened up to us a little more; our experience of love has been enriched, and our involvement in God's actions has been strengthened. And that's worth more than a breakfast plate of Koh-i-noors.

Some people's prayers need to be cut off at both ends and set fire to in the middle – D L Moody

6

LITTLE AND OFTEN

Many biographies of great Christians are counter-productive in the effect they have upon lesser mortals of a later generation. We read the biographies of these giants and wilt under them. Their early rising, their ardent and protracted times of devotion, the frequency and miraculous nature of the answers they received – often the result of these dramatic accounts is that many Christians of today feel crushed and somewhat accused in their own poor efforts.

We forget that the events recorded in a biography are necessarily compressed. High spots that took place over a period of decades are telescoped into a mere few chapters, and these tend to dazzle us. They need not do so, for prayer is a lifetime and not a collection of isolated experiences, however encouraging they may have been.

Nevertheless the words are starkly there in the New Testament:

'Pray at all times'
'Pray on every occasion as the Spirit leads'
'Be persistent in prayer'
'Keep on praying for us'

How can one ever rise to such a standard, and especially in what must be the most frenetically *active* era in the history of civilisation?

What interests me is that the busiest people do in fact appear to have time to pray. Go back to the Old Testament at the time of Nehemiah. He was Judah's governor, reformer and public works director, all rolled into one. One reels at the mindbending schedule ahead of him as with his companions, he faced the task of re-building the shattered walls of Jerusalem and indeed the life of the restored community. It might have been understandable for him to have let others do the praying. After all, was he not a public figure with plenty on his mind? But the Book of Nehemiah fairly reeks of prayer.

Interspersed with the accounts of the wall-building enterprise – the organization, the personnel, and the sinister intrigues that threatened the whole operation – we come upon little snippets of Nehemiah's prayer life. Asked by the King of Persia, 'What is it that you want?' we read that Nehemiah replied as follows: 'Then I prayed to the God of heaven, and I answered the King ...' (Neh. 2:4, 5). Or later, in the teeth of a political storm, the governor-cum-builder recognizes that 'they were all trying to frighten us .... But I prayed, "Now strengthen my hands"' (6:9). And this is from a man who was so physically stretched that, on his own testimony, 'I didn't take off my clothes even at night'! (4:23 GNB).

May we be forgiven, those of us who feel we are too busy to pray! Jacques Ellul asserts, 'I cannot say to myself, "I haven't ten minutes to devote to prayer, so it is useless to try." *Prayer creates its own required time.*'

'Pray at all times,' urged the apostle Paul. What did he mean? We must often have heard it said of someone, 'She's always coughing.' Similarly, it can be said of a Christian, 'She's always praying.'

Little and often, this is surely what is meant. Granted, a set time and place for prayer is a desirable thing, but let that not blind us to the countless opportunities in a day when incidents, problems and even idle thoughts can be elevated to the level of prayer. The name of an old friend flits into mind during the lunch break. Need that name drop back again into the memory's filing system without being lifted, even wordlessly, to God? A relation of

49

mine told me of the habit he had developed of focusing his thoughts upon God every time he passes through the entrance of his place of work. There are many occasions when a Christian can do this. There are also the times when he may not! Archbishop William Temple once warned, 'The bus-driver, wending his way in a double-decker down Oxford Street, ought *not* to be thinking about God.'

Prayer is a life, a relationship. It is something like the marriage relationship. There are times when a husband and wife may be sitting at opposite ends of the room, but something happens – and their eyes meet in an unspoken communication. Similarly, in the friendship with God – little and often – the habit is formed of catching the attention of the one to whom life and personality have been committed. It is not an introspective, guilt-ridden activity. It does not involve an intense, high-powered approach to life. It is not even a technique. It is something that becomes utterly natural.

O Lord,
let your ear be attentive
to the prayer of this your servant
and to the prayer of your servants
who delight in revering
your name.
Give your servant success today.

From a prayer of Nehemiah
(Nehemiah 1:11)

The first hour of waking is the rudder that guides the whole day – Henry Ward Beecher

7

GET A START ON THE DAY!

'Thank you, friends,' said the photographer, and his head disappeared once more under the black cloth. Fifteen pairs of eyes stared at the famous Mr. Abrahams, who had been taking pictures of the Keswick Convention speakers' team year after year in England's Lake District, as Christians gathered by the thousand for a week of fellowship and study.

'That camera was once dropped from the top of Helvellyn,' murmured one of the group who thought he knew the history of Mr. Abrahams and his photography.

'Skiddaw, surely, wasn't it?' chimed in another voice.

I didn't know. I didn't mind really. I was waiting, fascinated, for the puff of white smoke that I felt sure the camera would emit at any moment.

Mr. Abrahams' head came out from under the cloth. 'All look this way,' he commanded gently. There was a movement of his hand. No puff of white smoke. No click even, it seemed.

'That's all, friends, thank you.' Another Keswick photograph was safely in the bag.

I have sometimes thought that the rules for successful group photographs are very much the same as the guidelines for positive prayer.

Rule one: Be natural! Not so easy when you're standing shoulder to shoulder facing a camera, it's true. But it was Christ who, in speaking of prayer, never tired of reminding his listeners that they were approaching someone they could call their 'heavenly Father.' The relationship is a family one, and the approach is to be natural.

Rule two: Keep still! They're always saying it at the photography sessions. 'There's someone moving ... would you keep *still* please!'

Rule three: Look at the camera!' Would you face *this* way, please?'

The application to the life of prayer is very obvious. Take posture, for example. When we come to pray what should we do? Should we kneel, sit, walk, stand or lie down? I can think of people who do all five! The important question to ask is, 'How can I best *get still*, mentally and spiritually, to focus my entire self on God?' It might be a good idea to vary our posture when it comes to our daily times of prayer. Some people only have to kneel down by their bedside in order to fall fast asleep! Better in such cases, then, to stand for prayer, or to walk. However, many Christians feel that kneeling is by far the most appropriate posture to adopt when addressing Almighty God. This is a valid point. It is true that we can speak to God at any time, and in any circumstances – driving a car or taking a bath. He is, after all, our heavenly Father. But if all our praying was undertaken in this way, we could well slide into a casual 'God-is-my-best-pal' kind of attitude that makes neither for true worship and reverence, nor for the inner stillness that gives point and direction to the day.

It was indeed at the Keswick Convention years ago that I heard leading Bible teacher, John Stott, speak of the need for this kind of focus and concentration in prayer. He described what he called *the battle of the threshold*. While there is a very definite place for the spontaneous 'out of the top of your head' type of prayer, there is also a great call to be still and un-hurried as we attempt to break through the barriers to effective prayer that are often created by innumerable distractions. Our aim is to 'get over the threshold' into a sense of the more immediate presence of God, in our communication with him. Surely this is why, 'while it was still dark', Jesus would take himself off to a lonely place (Mark 1:35).

Get a start on the day, and begin it with God! It's easy to say. Never was there a generation which has found it harder to do. We go to bed so much later now. Two hundred years ago most law-abiding citizens were in bed by seven-thirty or eight at night. There was no electric light to extend their day. And telephones? T.V.? The tyranny of mobile phones and e-mails? Along with the motor car, they were as remote as the moon. And what can one say today to the family which lives on the edge of a motorway, or in an inner city area? To the shift worker whose dawn begins during the evening rush hour? To the early morning commuter?

'We know all these justifications so well,' writes Jacques Ellul. 'They rest upon a mistaken point of view! *Is not prayer precisely of itself peace, silence, strength, since it is a way of being with God?*' (italics mine).

Let me give an illustration. Sports followers are acquainted with the powers of concentration exhibited by outstanding athletes. Jack Nicklaus was once asked how he was able to stand up to the pressures of professional golf. He replied, 'When I leave one green a flash comes up in my mind, and I "see" the next hole filmed for me; I see my drive, where it is going to land. As I put the ball on the tee, I don't just see the golf ball, I see the little *number* on the golf ball. Crowds are out. The hazards are out. The weather is out. The newspapers, the television, the radio are out – everything except that number on the golf ball and the place that I am going to hit it.'

We have seen the same ability to concentrate, to 'focus', in world-class sprinters, or in such tennis greats as Pete Sampras, Lindsay Davenport and André Agassi. It is something of this phenomenon that Jacques Ellul is pointing us to when he says that prayer creates the very silence needed for prayer – 'in which a few seconds can have a very great time value.'

The *battle of the threshold*, then, is not a battle of time so much as a battle of *direction*, and hence depth. The promises of God help us here. Christ's followers are promised that in him they have a great 'High Priest' who has gone into the very presence of God, and that, for their part, they have only to approach God's throne in prayer to be assured of a welcome!

(Heb. 4:14-16). It is for this reason that to combine prayer with the reading of the Bible is so helpful, because of the power of the Bible to help the praying man or woman to *focus* thought upon God, albeit for a limited period of time, and despite the unavoidable distractions that may surround him.

Desirable, then, as solitude and quiet may be for prayer, they are not essentials. The stillness we look for is an inward stillness that can occupy the centre of our lives, even while a storm rages around us.

A vivid illustration of this principle came from a camp for political prisoners, run by one of the world's notorious regimes of the late twentieth century. Every day the warders required one of the prisoners to wade out into the vast sewer pit, into which the camp's sanitary waste flowed. The reasoning was that it took a man to keep the mass of filth moving towards its intended destination.

For this role, the most saintly man in the camp – a pastor – was chosen, and he undertook the task without protest. Morning by morning he would wade out into the middle of the stinking waste, and there he would have his quiet time. As he went about his work, the warders and prisoners would hear him singing at the top of his voice. As often as not, the song that he chose to accompany his devotions ran as follows:

I come to the garden alone,
While the dew is still on the roses;
And the voice I hear, falling on my ear,
The Son of God discloses.
And he walks with me, and he talks with me,
And he tells me I am his own;
And the joy we share, as we tarry there
None other has ever known.

Well ... if a quiet time with God can be held in these conditions, it can be held absolutely anywhere! Let us then beware of deciding in advance what the ideal conditions of prayer must be, and then giving up the attempt in resignation because we cannot 'get time', or 'get quiet'. Instead prayer must create its own conditions, and we may well find that what begins as a five-minute, pre-breakfast 'focus' grows, through its own impetus, into something more ambitious. It is up to today's generation of Christians to prove that you can live in a world far removed from the solitude of the garden of Eden, and still walk with God, in an inward tranquillity.

I remember seeing the advertisement for an Italian hotel, featured in a British Airways magazine. It read, 'This hotel is noted for its quiet and solitude. In fact crowds from all over the world flock here to enjoy its solitude!' That's our world today – with a vengeance! And as 'today people', we have responsibilities – we have to live in this world and shape it.

Part 2

THE HEART OF PRAYER

Great art thou, O Lord, and greatly to be praised; great is thy power, and thy wisdom is infinite.

Thee would we praise without ceasing.

Thou callest us to delight in thy praise, for thou hast made us for thyself, and our hearts find no rest until we rest in thee; to whom with the Father and the Holy Ghost all glory, praise and honour be ascribed, both now and for evermore. Amen.

St. Augustine, AD 354

O what a dull thing is life without religion! –
John Wesley

8

THE PLACE OF EMOTION

'The church provides the dullest experience going.' So declared one of Britain's leading disc jockeys some years ago. But there is a drawback in making pronouncements from the sidelines. The tendency is to miss the area where all the real action is taking place. And, as far as the Christian Church is concerned, a fair proportion of the action is in the realm of the unobservable! This is why the best way of getting the latest news in church circles is to turn up at the meeting for prayer! When we pray we are entering an altogether new dimension of experience.

'Get this right,' wrote Archbishop Donald Coggan about prayer, 'and the odds are that there will be growth, a certain serenity and joy which come from getting one's perspectives right, a certain large-mindedness and large-heartedness which can only come from companying with God.'

Here indeed is a wider dimension of life. In fact our whole horizon becomes altogether more *interesting* when we learn, through prayer, to keep God at the centre of the picture. And if life with him is thought by the by-standers to be *dull,* what is life without him like? Richard Wurmbrand of Romania is emphatic in his diagnosis:

> The atheist's Bible is boring. In fact it could not be otherwise. Nobody can be eloquent for atheism. Atheism is a denial. Who can write enthusiastically about a negation? Religion has inspired symphonies, paintings, statues, poetry. Atheism, by its very nature, could never have this impact. Atheism has no wings.

Prayer is the great test. Life can never be dull and flat, when we are in daily communication with the God of all creativity and salvation. How could it? There will always be the thrill of adventure opening up to those who are convinced that God uses the prayers of his people to bring about his will. At times the sheer excitement of it will threaten to send our emotions soaring.

I was on a visit to Melbourne in 1998 when Alec and Deirdre Baker, two Christians who work in the Middle East, told this story in my hearing. A church leader had appealed for the re-opening of an English-speaking church that had been shut down by the Arab authorities, and was told, 'Yes, we will grant you back the church, provided that you can find the original deeds'.

As the deeds had been granted to Queen Victoria as far back as 1841, the prospects of success looked very poor. But prayer was made, and the search began – under a man called Tom Hamblen, who worked with *Operation Mobilisation*.

– 'We were at our wit's end', he reported. 'We tried and tried, but we couldn't track down the deeds'.

One morning, walking up the steps of the local Archives office yet again, he was asked for money by a blind beggar.

– 'I gave him something', said Tom, 'and he asked "Who are you?" I replied, "I'm the man who's come to represent the English church."'

– 'Oh,' said the beggar. '*Are you looking for the deeds*?'

– 'Yes!' came the amazed reply.

– 'Well,' said the beggar, 'I know where they are.'

– '*You* know where they are? But how can that be?'

– 'Ah, I once used to work in the Archives

department. If I can come in with you, I'll lead you to them!'

The two men went up the steps and into the building, threaded their way through a labyrinth of corridors and passageways, and finally came to a dusty back room – and there they found a box, stamped with the year *1841*. They opened it, and inside ... devastation! The termites had destroyed every document in the box.

Except one. The Queen Victoria document, because of its important association, had evidently been treated with a special preservative. It alone had survived. Even the Muslims spoke of this discovery as a miracle. The church was duly re-opened. Talk of emotion! But all this came out of sustained prayer.

Emotional high spots and peaks there will be in the Christian's life with God. We are not, however, to rely on them, nor to imagine that emotional feelings can in any sense serve as an accurate chart of Christian growth and discipleship. A famous church leader many years ago warned, 'Beware, lest you make a Christ of your feelings and sensations!'.

And yet we do this very thing, time and again. Christian people will often say to a counsellor: 'The trouble is, when I prayed for forgiveness for my sins, I didn't really *feel* guilty at all!'

– 'But *were* you guilty?' comes the question.

– 'O yes, most certainly so! But I don't *feel* particularly sorry.'

– 'But you've admitted your guilt? *And stopped doing it*?'

– 'Yes, yes, of course.'

– 'Then that's all that really matters, isn't it? You did the one important thing that had to be done. You actually confessed that you *were* guilty, and you've stopped doing it. *That means you've repented.*'

Another mistake that is frequently made lies in our tendency to equate our emotional low periods with *spiritual* deterioration. It is a false assumption. Of course if we are out of step with God on some issue and are disobeying him, we are very likely to experience inward depression. But we must also realize that our moods and feelings depend very much upon such factors as physical health, changing circumstances and even the weather.

Emotion in prayer will vary from individual to individual. We should never try to compare our emotions and inner experiences with someone else's. People will react to a given set of factors in the most amazingly diverse ways. I remember sitting in a cinema once, watching a scene in *Lawrence of Arabia*, in which an unfortunate individual was being sucked inexorably to his death in the quicksands. My uppermost emotion, I think, was one of curiosity: how was the illusion created? By an unseen trap door ... by running the sequence backwards? The person in the next seat to me, however, was breathing quickly, hands tightly clenched on the arm rest, anxiously involved in the drama.

In our life with God, should we be surprised at the divergence of emotions and attitudes? Some people, when they are deeply moved, become very silent, others weep or sing. Many *feel* nothing at all. For some, the praise sessions – those moments of overflowing effervescence – are the only valid emotional experiences. But this is not really the case. Christianity is altogether more *interesting* than a life lived on the one level of exuberant praise alone. *A plateau existence is, in the last analysis, a dull existence, whatever the level of the plateau.* Certainly the Christian will learn to 'rejoice in the Lord always' – but this does not mean that there will never be tears. If we read the Psalms, we shall be confronted with a great kaleidoscope of human experiences – doubt, insecurity, anger, solitude, awe and wonder, deep disappointment and overflowing thankfulness. It's all there. And the very *absence* of feeling and emotion – that, too, is an *experience!* All these have their place in the life of prayer.

Has the point sunk home by now? Never let us despise our emotions – they are a vital part of *life!* But let us understand their place in our relationship to God. They will fluctuate, and we should not expect the bonuses of one day necessarily to last till the next. Let us not seek for emotional experiences in themselves, when they do not already exist. Such things should not be created artificially. And let it be realized that in the whole history of mankind, there has never been anyone quite like *you!* To long for someone else's experience is only to devalue and even to deny your own unique identity.

Today's is the era of *experience*. We are wrong to shelve this dimension as unimportant. But if I were asked to name *the* experience which, above all, was the one which gave satisfaction and fulfilment, I would give this reply. It's the experience of having found the truth – the truth about myself and my role on planet Earth, the truth about my relationship to the universe, and the truth about God. I know of no greater experience in all of life.

On one hand you can resist the Lord's will, and on the other hand you can run ahead before his will is clear – Gottfried Osei-Mensah of Ghana

9

HOT LINE?

'The Lord has told me to give a message in the main meeting later this morning. At what time would you like me to report to the platform?' It was during a European youth event in Brussels some years ago that I was approached in this way by a delegate from one of the thirty-nine countries represented.

I was programme chairman of the event, and so was faced by requests of this kind, not once, but many times. We could probably have filled the programme with those who informed me that God had told them to give a message from the platform.

In this case I thanked my questioner for coming. 'You feel that God wants you to speak? Then in coming to have a word with me you've discharged your responsibilities. Are you willing to leave the arrangement of the programme in our committee's hands now?'

'If I do not speak, you are responsible at the Judgement!' flashed back my questioner. And there we had to leave the matter.

The Lord has told me. Undoubtedly the majority of people who interpret their actions with these words do so sincerely. Nevertheless such an approach amounts to a form of spiritual blackmail. Because their actions are attributed to the direct instructions of God, the rest of us are supposed to accede to their requests, simply on the basis of an unauthenticated claim. I have even heard of a member of a certain Christian group who announced to his fellow members that he had had a word of 'prophecy' from the Lord that he was to be the new group chairman. Meekly the rest of the fellowship let him have his way, and appointed him without question!

There is no infallible, personal hot-line to God that stands above the considered views of other Christians. Nor is the guidance of God irrational or mechanistic. Our relationship with God in prayer is that of children to their Father, not that of a robot to a computer, or an animal to its master. Psalm 32:8, 9 states the biblical position:

> *The Lord says, 'I will instruct you and teach you in the way you should go; I will counsel you and watch over you. Do not be like the horse or the mule, which have no understanding but must be controlled by bit and bridle or they will not come to you.'*

God's guidance is there all right, but it is not unintelligent, mindless guidance. Horses and mules do not have the use of understanding that we do. God will teach us his way, but we are to co-operate with the full use of our minds, enlightened as they should be with a prayerful study of the Bible. In the pursuit of a career we will have a number of biblical principles to guide us, but the detailed application will have to be left to us. Jobs will not simply fall into our lap – we will have to search them out. By all means let us pray about our holidays, but not then sit back passively and 'wait to see where Jesus directs us', as some have done.

All this means that our attitude towards God's guidance is humble, ever open to the correction available from Scripture, Christian friends and altered circumstances. When I was made a minister, I was asked, as part of the ordination ceremony, whether I felt called by God to this position. My answer was required to be, 'I think so'.

I think so. Nothing more definite? After all the training and study that has been involved, after every check and balance has been brought to bear upon the candidate? After the bevy of advisers, clergy and selectors that had looked me over? *I think so*. The answer is a humble one, and really very scriptural!

That is one tendency, then, to which we are prone – the bland assumption that prayer to God will give us a push-button type of guidance. Another tendency is to make our praying a cover for disobedience or delay, where God's will is already plainly clear. It can be summed up in the sentence, *I prayed about it.* Take the cases of Balaam in the Old Testament.

Balaam was a prophet of great oratorical gifts and spiritual leadership. Balak, King of the Moabites, and a sworn enemy of Israel, was resolved to persuade Balaam to bring a curse on Israel. If necessary he would bribe him.

> *But Balaam answered them, 'Even if Balak gave me his palace filled with silver and gold, I could not do anything great or small to go beyond the command of the Lord my God'* (Num. 22:18).

So far so good. But in the next breath, Balaam destroys his own credibility!

> *'Now stay here tonight as the others did, and I will find out what else the Lord will tell me'* (Num. 22:19).

What is he proposing? He's going to go and 'pray about it'! Here lay the seeds of Balaam's eventual downfall. He had already been forbidden even to accompany Balak's men (22:12). The end of the story finds him with a foot miserably in both camps, journeying along with Balak and yet not able to bring himself to curse Israel. It is a common occurrence.

There have been numerous cases, in Christian history, of people 'praying' as to whether they should compromise in business or entangle themselves in an immoral relationship in the face of the clear Bible teaching on these matters. There is no 'hot line' to God that will over-ride his own word. 'Instead of quitting sin and mourning over it,' said C H Spurgeon, 'some men talk of praying.' Prayer can be used as a cover for many unworthy actions. Gossip is one such. 'I'm telling you this about so-and-so – in the strictest confidence of course – *for your prayers.*' Before long everybody knows the dark story, simply because God's people indulged themselves and couldn't keep their mouths shut!

One of our grandchildren was given a clockwork toy for Christmas. You wound it up and placed it on the floor and it would then whizz frantically around, haphazardly and in any direction. You couldn't predict what it would do next. Some people's guidance is like that clockwork toy. The Lord is telling them this, that and the other. Yes, they've prayed about it. But three weeks later sees an abrupt reversal of their actions. They're off in another direction, still, supposedly, guided by God.

God does not guide people by fits and starts. Nor does he treat us as automata. His guidance is a steady thing, that grows in the heart of a praying individual. But he provides constant correctives. These are the God-given checks of Scripture, the Christian mind and good friends. The humble child of God ought to be able to gently push open the door of opportunity and say with trustful confidence, *I think so*.

O Lord God
of Abraham, Isaac and Israel,
Let it be known today
that you are God in Israel,
and that I am your servant
and have done all these things
at your command.

*(From Elijah's prayer,
1 Kings 18:36)*

One of the saddest things about the atheist is that he has no one to thank – Hugh Silvester

10

GRACIAS!

I once attended a dinner in The Painted Hall at the Royal Naval College, Greenwich. During it my attention was drawn to the intricate painting executed by Sir James Thornhill.

Actually that is a major understatement, because the entire hall *is* a painting. Sir James had really given it his all! The ceiling and walls are covered by the most exotic and extravagant representations of cherubs and figures, both historical and mythical, all completed in the Baroque manner by Sir James between the years 1707 and 1726. There was Queen Anne and her consort; Old Father Time dominated another area; the family of George I occupied the end wall. Nineteen years is a fair chunk of one's life to give to a work of this kind, and my eyes kept straying up from my soup to another and yet another aspect of this incredible painting. Last of all the artist had evidently painted himself. There he was, on the end wall, just near George I, staring straight at the viewer. He didn't look too happy, I had to admit.

Then it was pointed out to me that Sir James Thornhill had received rather meagre thanks for his herculean labours, besides which he had been inadequately paid. His self-portrait was a delicious example of oblique reproach; his left hand can be seen curled, half-open, behind his back, in the manner of one expecting a tip! It was the perfect postscript to years of hard slog.

Thank you! Gracias! Danke! Tack sa mycket! Webale! Wherever you find yourself in the world, it is as well to find out the local way of saying *Thank you.* This is basic. It is the mark of an educated person, of someone who has learnt the common courtesies. Yes, they have to be taught, as anyone knows who has had the responsibility of bringing up children.

Because gratitude is not natural to us, it actually has to be *commanded*, when we come to the Bible. 'Be thankful' the apostle Paul instructs his readers (Col. 3:15). This is no optional extra to Christian discipleship. It comes in a list of basic characteristics of the new life; compassion, kindness, humility, gentleness, patience, forgiveness and love. And then, thankfulness.

Gratitude does not spring naturally to the forefront of our minds. It bubbles over, of course, when the news is distinctly good, when a crisis is safely over, or a handsome gift has just arrived. Too often, if it is gratitude, it is of the mushroom variety, here for a day and then quickly fading. Paul the apostle had learned something deeper:

> *I have learned to be content whatever the circumstances. I know what it is to be in need and I know what it is to have plenty. I have learned the secret of being content in any and every situation, whether well fed or hungry, whether living in plenty or in want (Phil. 4:11, 12).*

That Paul had truly earned the right to say this there can be no doubt about. The words were not written by a hotel window, but in prison. Elsewhere he urges, 'Be joyful always; pray continually; give thanks in all circumstances' (1 Thess. 5:16, 17).

I have often noticed that the people who appear to express the greatest degree of gratitude are those who have the hardest times in life. Perhaps it is that adversity teaches us this Christian grace. There are people around who have amply demonstrated that you can find reasons for thankfulness, even in the most miserable environment. I remember carrying out some house-to-house visiting in south-east

London years ago. At one household I was confronted by arrogance and hardness, brazen prosperity; the complacent attitude of 'We have everything we need'. And then the parting shot on the doorstep, 'In any case, what about all the suffering in the world, if there's a God of love?' I felt like a whipped dog.

How different was the very next house! They were poor people and the place was somewhat down-at-heel. One of the children had a crippled foot, and had experienced months of life in a hospital. Yet everywhere there were the hallmarks of true love, and of deep gratitude. It overflowed our conversation and was even visible in the Christian books I noticed when I walked in. These things were not manufactured. They are the by-products of the Gospel.

And if we have the Gospel, then we can – and must – practise this habit of expressing gratitude. 'God save little children from a prayerless home!' exclaimed Gipsy Smith, the preacher of old. A society has become gross, when children are brought up to take for granted all that comes their way – their home, their friends, their clothes and their toys – as though the world owed them these gifts. Consumerism is their mindset. Thankfulness is rarely expressed. They have a rude shock coming to them before many years.

There is not enough praise and thanksgiving in Christian circles generally, and we should be grateful for those who have shown us the way. The apostle Paul was not the only Christian to learn to give praise in prison. Take Corrie ten Boom, the Dutch Christian. She became known to millions through *The Hiding Place*, the book and the film of her experiences in Ravensbrück concentration camp. Her Christian witness during World War II was an inspiration to many.

> The fleas! This was too much. 'Betsie, there's no way even God can make me grateful for a flea.'
>
> '"Give thanks in all circumstances,"' she quoted. 'It doesn't say, "in pleasant circumstances". Fleas are part of this place where God has put us.'
>
> (*The Hiding Place*, Hodder and Stoughton)

It is only later in the book that the freedom of the two women to hold Bible services for the other prisoners is seen as resulting directly from the guards' reluctance to enter the huge, flea-infested quarters!

The message of such experiences, and of the Bible is, 'Think again before grumbling in adverse circumstances. Look around, and see whether there isn't some element present for which to give praise to God.'

I do not mean that there is no place for tears. 'Weep with those who weep,' urges Paul in Romans 12:15. Sure enough, there have been well-meaning Christian people around who have forgotten this when confronted by personal tragedy among their friends, and too easily say 'Praise the Lord!' when they ought to be weeping! They have achieved little, beyond devaluing the currency of praise. The Corrie ten Boom pattern is the biblical one, where tears and praise often join hands. You can be in tears, following bereavement or a marriage tragedy, and yet through the sorrow, still manage to give thanks to God for that visitor, for the neighbour who volunteered to help with the shopping, for the uplift of praying friends. It is a healthy thing when we can wake to every new day with thankfulness and praise to God as a vital part of our praying.

In a sermon many years ago, Dr. Paul Rees put forward his mandate for gratitude:

If thankfulness arises through prosperity, well and good. But what are you going to do when the prosperity fails? If thankfulness springs up through health, well and good. But what will you do when disease makes you bedridden? Must you then become glum or bitter? *But now*, supposing it is *through our dear Lord Christ* that you cultivate the fine art of thanksgiving, then what? Then money in the bank, however useful, does not have me at its mercy: if I lose it I can still offer thanks.

'Through Christ.' This is what Paul advocates, when he uses the phrase 'give thanks *through him* to God the Father.' It is not a cheap thing to say that a person who has encountered the Gospel has every reason to give thanks in all circumstances. It is not a trite saying, that if you have Christ in your life you have everything. Simply because there are plenty of people who are proving, even in hard times the truth of this principle and they are all around us. You know them when you meet them, because they never grumble about *anything!*

Meditation is the soul's chewing – William Grimshaw

11

PREACH YOURSELF A SERMON

Ever tried preparing a sermon? Perhaps not. But have you ever tried preparing a sermon for your own consumption? This is roughly what Christian meditation is. It is allied to prayer, but distinct from it. It has been defined as 'an activity of thought, while prayer is the rejection of every thought'. Which, when you think about it, is true. When praying, you are engaged in a battle against the *intrusion* of outside thoughts, so that full concentration may be given to God.

But in meditation, thought plays a very full part. Most westerners don't really know how to use silence. There is a constant clattering around us for much of the day. We find ourselves chattering and talking, as though life were one great cocktail party. Indeed there are many who are such compulsive and opinionated talkers that by their very garrulity they shut themselves out of God's kingdom, never giving themselves a chance to stop, listen and *think*.

We are so conditioned that for much of the time our thoughts are knocking haphazardly around, like bumper cars at a funfair. Meditation is the art of channelling thought in a single direction. It is very productive. Back in the seventeenth century, Sir Isaac Newton, when praised for his great contribution to our understanding of the universe, remarked, 'I had no special sagacity – only the power of patient thought.' He made his discoveries, he said, 'by keeping a subject constantly before me until the first dawnings open little by little into the full light.'

The Kikuyu people of Kenya have a good word to describe this activity. It is the word *meciria* (mesheeria). By it is meant more than simply *thoughts*. It means *thoughts with a difference*, directed, powerful, *original* thoughts.

Bring this into the Christian context, and we're talking of a kind of applied thinking which has changed and shaped society repeatedly in the last two thousand years. For by Christian meditation we mean reflection and thought which is channelled and guided by God. The journalist, Malcolm Muggeridge, once made the point that the most vital elements in the Christian story are those which, over the centuries, have stemmed from dissidence rather than agreement. Luther and Wesley arc prime examples of this phenomenon. Here were leaders – and there have been many like them – who were able to pick up a seed thought, absorb it, study it and then communicate it – even against the established thinking of the time – and society was changed as a result.

How can we ensure that the seed thought is truly from God? We are right to be wary of the many meditation groups that have mushroomed around the world in the last few years. It is possible to lose your own identity and to fall prey to strange and even demonic powers by the *thoughtless* opening of your mind. And the technique, advocated in Transcendental Meditation, of reciting a meaningless word to oneself, implies the absence of true relationship, the absence of any real personality in God himself. Christ's way is to resist the technique of reciting mantras as a way to God. 'When you pray,' he urged, 'do not keep on babbling like pagans' (Matt. 6:7). Meditation should never take place in a vacuum.

Your thinking is like your radio listening. Tuning is required. And while *technique* is not of the essence, nevertheless we value a few familiar landmarks on the radio dial – even if

only the X of *Luxembourg,* or the Y of *Sony.*
Similarly in meditation, we need a few handles
to grab hold of. Without those handles our
thoughts are undisciplined and unproductive.
One married couple I knew, both fresh to the
Christian faith, began with Bible page
numbers. 'That was a nice bit, Brian, on page
240 of the Bible!' It was only later that they got
into the swing of books, chapters and verses.

How then do you meditate? You take a
thought from the Bible. It may have occurred
in a passage from your regular reading of the
Bible. It stands out somewhat from the page.
You take it and begin to 'chew' it over in your
mind. It may not be a hefty chunk, perhaps only
a sentence, a word sometimes.

'I thirst.' I remember meditating on this
phrase one Good Friday. It was spoken by our
Lord, while he was dying on the cross. I tried
to let my mind revolve around these words,
much as one might walk round a chandelier,
picking out first one shaft of colour and then
another as a different facet presented itself. The
agony of dying in a sun-baked city in the
Middle East, exposed to the crowd, the
hostility, the flies. The reflection that he had
chosen this way, in accordance with the
Father's will, so that the scriptures from Psalm
22 might be fulfilled.

My strength is gone,
Gone like water spilt on the ground.
All my bones are out of joint;
My heart is like melted wax.
My throat is as dry as dust
And my tongue sticks to the roof of my mouth.

Anything else about Christ, and thirst? Yes, he had come to satisfy people's thirst. Wasn't it somewhere in John's Gospel? Hadn't I heard a sermon on it? ... The woman at the well! Jesus had said to her, 'Whoever drinks the water I give him will never thirst' (John 4:14). And now here *he* was ... thirsty. Then, Good Friday's message is that by his dying thirst, Christ provides a way of satisfying the thirst of the world. Thirst ... for what? I remembered a biography I'd once read about the evangelist George Whitefield. As a young man, searching desperately for peace of mind and soul, he'd recalled the words 'I thirst', and reflected that they were uttered just before Christ's own anguish came to an end. Whitefield himself had cried out in helpless despair, 'I thirst!' – and peace, forgiveness and integration had flooded in.

Thirst ... Do Christians thirst? I remembered reading another biography – about D L Moody who, although committed as a Christian leader, was thirsting for more of Christ's Spirit and filling in his life. He found fulfilment at the hands of Christ. A sentence from the biography floated hazily back into my mind: 'The dead dry days were gone. I was all the time tugging and carrying water. *But now I have a river that carries me.*' Lord, if you can do that for the woman you met at the well, if you can do it for Whitefield and for Moody, then you can do it today. Thank you for the thirst you endured – for *me*.

What was I doing? Preaching a sermon on two words only, just to myself. And now it was beginning to turn into prayer. I find that a helpful pattern of Christian meditation. It need not be a prolonged activity at all. Two, perhaps three minutes are enough, initially. These can grow naturally into something rather longer as progress is made. Such 'seed thoughts' can be taken into the day, and meditated upon yet again at different moments. Indeed, they can help to shape the very day itself – and the life.

I once heard an eminent psychiatrist give a lecture. Some seventy of us were listening to him. He told us the therapy he suggests for many of his patients is an exercise in Christian meditation last thing at night before dropping off to sleep. A seed thought, like a nightcap, something to reflect on, something that can, even during sleep, get to work upon the subconscious.

'You know the uncanny way in which you can so often will yourself to wake up early, simply by instructing yourself the night before?' he challenged. 'It's the same principle here. I tell my patients to chew over the selected phrase from the Bible as they drift off to sleep. First thing in the morning – there it is again. *It's been with them all night.* I wouldn't claim that they all turned into devout Christians. But one thing I've noticed in countless instances. If they kept up the pattern night after night, their whole disposition and outlook at the end of a month was radically, even magically, improved.'

But it's not magic, really. James 1:21 states the principle clearly. 'Accept the word planted in you, which can save you.' The King James version uses the phrase – '*the engrafted word*, which is able to save your souls'. Engrafted – that's precisely it. It becomes a part of our life and character. *Meciria*. Deep thoughts, life-changing creative thoughts. It's the same thing.

Don't think the manifestations are going to feed you. They are given to shake you up – to drive you to the Bread of Life itself – Festo Kivengere of Uganda

12

BROCA'S AREA

'What about speaking in tongues?' a girl of eighteen once said to me. 'It does seem to be in the Bible!' True, and we should be grateful for this fact. How puzzled we would be if it were *not* featured in the Bible! One hears of the phenomenon of praying in an unintelligible language in other religions and cultures. It occurs with Hinduism and spiritistic circles. In ancient Greece the utterances of the Oracle at Delphi were supposedly given under special inspiration. It would be strange if there were not found, within Christianity, some kind of God-given counterpart.

Admittedly 'praying in tongues', as such, is not heavily emphasized in the Bible. There is no evidence that Jesus ever prayed in this way. Out of the twenty-seven books of the New Testament, only two make mention of this ability. This is not to downgrade a valid gift intended by God for some, though not for all (1 Cor. 12:29, 30), but to see it in its right place, that of secondary importance in Christian experience.

Actually it is only in comparatively recent times that we have taken much notice of the centre for articulate speech in the human mind, known since 1861 as 'Broca's area' and situated, as the experts tell us, *'in the third frontal convolution of the dominant cerebral hemisphere'!* It is this centre which can respond to certain kinds of stimulation – religious or indeed merely psychological – so causing a person to utter words. Thus, far from being a highly 'unnatural' phenomenon, it is directly related to the very physiology of our being. We should be grateful, then, for the Bible record, in that it shows us that non-Christian cultures have no monopoly of tongue-speaking, but that God's Holy Spirit can enter the realm of Broca's area and bring even out of that one of his gifts!

'I can understand the significance of the tongues at Pentecost,' someone might object. *'They* were telling of the wonderful works of God and instead of being *un*intelligible, they were clear. The bystanders were able to understand every word, each in his own language. There was a point to that! But what about the later occurrences, when the languages were *not* understood? Such an ability seems to be of limited value.'

Precisely. It is indeed of value, in its

Christian connections, but not of *immense* value. It receives limited emphasis in the New Testament. In fact we would never have known that the apostle Paul was able to pray with strange languages, had he not actually mentioned it. He revealed this fact in order to correct the excesses in the church at Corinth, a fellowship which, in its immaturity, had got the gift of tongues out of proportion. Paul deals with the problem positively. As far as the gift of tongues is concerned he can out-do the lot of them – but ...!

> *I thank God that I speak in strange tongues much more than any of you. But in church worship I would rather speak five words that can be understood, in order to teach others, than speak thousands of words in strange tongues. Do not be like children in your thinking, my brothers (I Cor. 14:18-20 GNB).*

But. This is the word of correction, and it is the important word in any study of this section on the gifts of the Spirit. Too often people overlook the 'buts'. Here are a few of them:

> *I may be able to speak the languages of men and even of angels, but if I have no love, my speech is no more than a noisy gong ... (13:1).*

The one who speaks in strange tongues helps only himself, but the one who proclaims God's message helps the whole church (14:4). I would like all of you to speak in strange tongues, but I would rather that you had the gift of proclaiming God's message (14:5). What should I do, then? I will pray with my spirit, but I will pray also with my mind (14:15).

It is important to understand that, in these passages, Paul is not giving basic Christian teaching on the gifts of the Spirit, in a kind of 'neutral' situation. Here was a church that was already enthusiastic about these gifts, particularly the more unusual variety. 'I would like you all to speak in tongues,' he affirms. *They were anyway!* The brunt of his message is contained in the 'but' that follows.

Thus there is a value, even if a limited value, in the ability – given by God to some – to pray in a strange language, thereby by-passing the usual thinking processes. The value of the gift centres largely in its private use, emphasizes Paul. He does not define the value beyond using the word 'helping' or 'edifying'. He is then quick to add that *'I will pray also with my mind.'*

For the person to whom God has given this

ability, there will be no problems, then, if the biblical rules of health are kept! Praying in tongues is to be seen chiefly as something between you and God alone. You should not be distressed if at any time the ability leaves you. God, the giver, knows best, and he can be trusted. See to it that this gift, as with any ability God may give you, never becomes your Gospel. You may feel tempted to enthuse about your gift in the presence of others, even to urge that your fellow-Christians should pray in the same way as yourself. Once you do that, you are in danger of starting a 'tongues movement'!

For the person upon whom God has other gifts to bestow, these are not problems once you remember that *gifts are to be given and not grabbed*. Let me reassure you: every Christian, without exception, has at least one gift! 'The same God gives ability to everyone for their particular service' (1 Cor. 12:6). Let no fellow-believer, however sincere and good, ever pressurize you into thinking that because you do not possess a certain gift, you are somehow deficient in your Christian experience. Never let yourself become dazzled by the supposed gifts of others. Instead discover and use the gifts God *has* given you.

And to him be all the glory.

After my first operation, finding I would have long hours just lying in bed, I said to myself, 'Good. Now I will employ this time in intercession and prayer.' But to my surprise and alarm I found I could not! – Isobel Kuhn

13

THE TIMES WHEN NOT TO PRAY

A girl candidate being interviewed for a Christian society that must be nameless was asked this misguided question: 'There has been a mining disaster. People have been killed. A woman's dead husband has just been brought to the pithead. What text would you give her?'

What text would you give her? Such a time and such a moment is hardly the occasion for opening Bibles and kneeling in prayer. You put your arms round the newly-bereaved widow, and stay with her. A strong cup of tea will be a help. A doctor may be necessary. For some time to come people ought to be willing to do her shopping for her. Few people want to go to the shops and face the world when they've just been bereaved. Practical help of this kind will be of more value than any amount of 'spiritual' help, books on bereavement and so on. Indeed, in this context, the practical *is* the spiritual. This is God's way, so often, when comforting the sorrowing and the depressed.

Remember the story of Elijah in 1 Kings 19, just after the great triumph on Mount

Carmel over the prophets of Baal? Suddenly reaction sets in, and there is Elijah, the greatest prophet of the Old Testament, fleeing from a woman, fearful and depressed. "'I have had enough, Lord," he said, "Take my life'" (1 Kings 19:4). What does God do? Tell him to pray more? Swamp him with a deluge of God-talk? No. The super-spiritual approach is useless in the helping of a depressive. The remedy comes in terms of the physical, first of all. Some sleep and then a meal (19:5). And then some more sleep. After that, another meal! And then? Something to do. Something practical. Anoint Jehu King of Israel (19:16).

Moses felt just the same earlier on, when suffering from 'People Shock' back in Numbers 11:14. 'I can't be responsible for all these people by myself; it's too much for me! If you are going to treat me like this, take pity on me and kill me....' And God's care for Moses comes in terms of providing others to help him in his task. Or there was Jonah who, after the success of his preaching, folds up. 'Now Lord, let me die. I am better off dead than alive' (Jonah 4:3). God cares for him too. He provides a shelter for him, so giving him an opportunity for reflection and counsel.

'I've prayed and prayed about my problem!' people sometimes tell me. Frequently, all they have succeeded in doing is to *pray the problem further in*. Especially is this so in the case of emotional problems or besetting sins. By all means let such people be encouraged to pray, but to focus more on other issues than those encompassed by their own horizon. Let them look outward, at the needy world around them. This will give balance to their prayer life and prevent them becoming marooned on the desert island of 'my problem'.

Someone who is not well, physically, may well be low emotionally, and we should not be surprised if this is so. People often worry when they find they cannot pray in hospital. But they shouldn't. Concentration is at a low ebb, and energy is in short supply. Others may pray for them, but they need not pray themselves. In such cases, sluggishness in the prayer life has more to do with the physical than the spiritual realm. At the onset of mental conflict or depression, too, it ought to be recognized that there may well be different diagnoses for these experiences. All too often, well-meaning Christian people assume that *all* depression has a spiritual root and must be treated accordingly. But this is not so. To pour on the prayer may not be the answer. Often, what is most needed is the friendly presence of someone who is prepared to listen. But let's move on further.

'There come times,' writes O Hallesby, *'when I have nothing more to tell God.'* This is a common experience. We have told God what is on our mind, and it only seems like pointless repetition to tell him all over again. In that case, let it rest in a companionable silence between ourselves and him. Silence is frequently a sign of friendship and trust. There are some people we cannot easily be silent with. We feel that every second ought to be filled with talk and chatter. We are nervous in case silence descends – the awkward empty silence when two people have nothing in common. How often have we enjoyed times of silent companionship with God? When there is nothing in particular that we want to say to him because it's already been said? We should welcome these occasions when the silence of trust and friendship descends between ourselves and him. Let it happen! We shall find that such silences are like those that spring up naturally between good friends – the silences that we would like to *prolong*.

There are also the times when, in praying for relatives, we simply do not know what to pray *for?* We have grown out of the childhood 'Bless Mum and Dad, my sister and me; us four and no more' type of prayer. Even so there may be nothing specific on our minds. A missionary once told me that in such cases he tries to 'ponder each person in turn before God. I try to surround them with love and affection; wishing them well in Christ. Often there isn't more to do than just that.'

Let me not close this chapter without asking a last question. Is there a Christian reader going through a time of uncertainty and darkness at the time these pages are being turned? When, for one of various reasons, you simply are not able to articulate any prayer to God, and you feel you are entering a never-ending tunnel? True, you may not be able to pray during this period, but anchor yourself to the thought expressed by the psalmist of old: 'Darkness and light are the same to you' (Ps. 139:12). God will be there too, in the darkness just as much as he ever was when you were walking in the clear daylight. Yours can be, temporarily, the experience of Moses of old, related in Exodus 20:21, 'Moses approached the thick darkness, *where God was*'. Or, as the diminutive missionary, Gladys Aylward, once scribbled in the margin of her Bible:

Lonely! The very word can start the tears ...
Who walk with Christ can never walk alone.
Alone, but not alone.
He is here.

Part 3

THE WORK OF PRAYER

O Lord, let us not live to be useless;
For Christ's sake. Amen.

John Wesley, 1703

I hope the Lord takes highest delight in elderly grandmothers in nursing homes who didn't dwell on their plight, but rather prayed, without fanfare, for others – Joni Eareckson Tada

14

THE REAL WORKERS

'I pray for you on the nineteenth day of every month,' an overseas Christian leader once told me. I was staggered – and at the same time humbled. To think that this busy man, with all the duties of his work on top of him, could bother to include in his prayers someone he rarely saw, and who was several thousand miles away in any case – that indicates real belief in the power of prayer! But then the top men and women in God's kingdom are like that. They had it all worked out years ago, and they continue to revise and work on their prayer lists or intercession diaries, taking prayer seriously and touching a vast collection of far-flung people through the power stemming from their private times with God.

Top men and women? No, we don't really talk like that in Christian circles. We don't, because we have too many reminders, from the Bible, of God's disconcerting habit of reversing the placings! The last shall be first, and the first last. So, not Eliab – the obvious choice – when it came to choosing a new King for Israel, but little David, who hadn't even been invited to the selection parade! 'The Lord does not look at the things man looks at. Man looks at the outward appearance, but the Lord looks at the heart' (1 Sam. 16:7).

It will be established one day, all too clearly, just who the 'top people' were, in God's estimation. We may well find, at the end of time, when the scales are finally weighed, that those people who had *really* carried the work of God were a great army of people that we never knew anything about – people unnoticed by the world at large, but singled out for the one thing they had in common: they took God and his kingdom seriously.

This is not to imply that lists of names and prayer diaries are essentials if prayer is to be taken seriously. Many people can't use them at all. But it is worth asking, 'If a "mechanical" list is not for me, what *is* right?' After all, the apostle Paul reels off a great list of men and women at the end of his letter to the Romans. They were evidently to the forefront of his mind whenever he thought about the Christians at Rome, and he had a prayerful concern for them. But up to the time of writing his letter he had never, as a Christian, visited Rome even once! Yet the names spill out: Ampliatus, Urbanus and Stachys, Apelles, Aristobulus,

Herodion and Narcissus, Tryphena and Tryphosa – all these, and more, clearly claimed a slice of Paul's prayers. And this from only *one* of the many churches with which he had a link.

Somebody once told me about the *rule of thumb* way of remembering the different categories of people needing prayer. You start with your thumb itself. That, being closer to your body than any of your fingers, reminds you to pray for your nearest friends and relations. Then comes your forefinger, which is what you point and *instruct* with. Here you remember to pray for those who have authority over you in some way: the boss, your teachers, your minister. After that, comes the big finger, the 'important' people, those in authority, those who wield the power nationally, these are the VIP's – and they include men and women who have given their whole lives to God's service, here or in another land altogether. After that comes the finger which they always say is the 'weak' finger; you can't do much with that second to last finger, and so you turn to prayer on behalf of the weak and disadvantaged, people in hospital, the undernourished and the refugees of the world. Last of all comes the little finger, representing, inevitably, little you! It's only a start, but if you have no established pattern for prayer at all, start here!

There is a wonderful society called the London City Mission, responsible for the placing of full-time 'missionaries' in a strategic area of the capital. I remember meeting one such missionary, Lional Ball by name. He was responsible for visiting the theatres of the West End, but his journeys also brought him into the Old Bailey, where over the years so many criminals have been brought to justice. From time to time he would go, armed with the Gospel, into the sex shops of Soho, to share something of God's love with the management. I asked if I could have the London City Mission prayer calendar, laid out with names and needs, a few for every day of the month. He promised to fix this for me, and added, 'Whenever my name comes up on the calendar, you can be sure I don't waste a minute of that day. On that day, more than any other, I spend the whole day out visiting my beat, knowing that I have the prayers of hundreds of people behind me!'

I come myself from a missionary family. Some years ago my father was asked to address a missionary gathering in Great Yarmouth. He went and spoke about the challenges and encouragements of the Church in East Africa, where he had laboured for some twenty years, and where I spent my childhood. At the end of the meeting, two diminutive, rather elderly, ladies approached him.

'We said to each other before the meeting that we wouldn't come and speak to you,' one admitted.

'But then,' chipped in the other, 'we felt we just had to come and have a word with you.'

'You see,' resumed the first lady, 'although we've never met you before, we know all about you, and we've got your picture at home. In fact we've got a whole room of missionary clippings and photos, given to this ministry.'

'The thing is,' interrupted her companion once more, 'we've been praying for you and all the members of your family every day, since the moment we saw in the missionary magazine that you were going to serve God in East Africa. *So you don't mind us having a word with you, do you?*'

If there were such categories as 'top people' in the Christian Church, these individuals would be among them. We shall surely discover, when the final issues come to light at the last day, that they, and people like them, did more than anyone else to carry the work of God upon their shoulders.

The work? 'We have actually got it all wrong,' said Eric Alexander of Scotland, 'when we speak as we do about "praying for the work", because prayer *is* the work!'

It seems that God made us to expect life to be exciting – Luis Palau

15

PRAYING FOR A MIRACLE

'I can work miracles,' said the man sitting in a circle of Bible students.

The speaker had come into the study group as a stranger, in one of England's leading cities. Now it transpired, on his own admission, that he was a worker with occult forces and black magic. And there he was – in a Bible study group!

'What can Christianity do?' he challenged the group. 'Can you work a miracle in front of me now? Show me what you can do!'

Supposing you had been in that group of Christians. What would you have done? Attempted to compete with black magic? Called down fire from above? Spoken in tongues? Performed a healing? In this case the church's pastor was present. Magnificently he rose to the challenge – in the New Testament way.

'Yes,' he replied firmly. 'There is something that can be done. *I'm going to pray that Christ will liberate you from the bondage of Satan, and set you free.'* And this very thing happened. Within a week the worker in black magic had changed sides and had become a Christian! This was related to me by one of the pastor's relations.

This is the whole point about the power of living Christianity. It was never given us for the performance of sensations. It is available for the work of God, so that the lives of men and women can be turned around and brought into friendship with himself once more. And if there are miracles they tend to be incidental to the main story line.

The student of the Bible will realize that there is a pattern about the occurrence of miracles in the Old and New Testaments. Miracles tend to come in batches. And the reason for that is that a miracle doesn't occur simply for its own sake. *It comes as a sign of something more important.* It is noticeable that in John's Gospel the miracles of Christ were referred to as 'signs' pointing to his identity.

Bible miracles seem to coincide with every new stage in the giving of God's revelation as though to *authenticate* the new revelation, and the messengers, as being truly of God. The first great profusion of miracles features in the stories of Moses, the great lawgiver. Here is the first major era in the biblical revelation –

that of the giving of the Law. Then comes a gap, in which far fewer miracles are recorded. But as we move on to the era of the prophets, and particularly Elijah, the outstanding Old Testament prophet, another great rush of miracles heralds the new stage of God's revelation. Another gap follows – indeed hundreds of years would pass, with no recorded miracles. But move into the New Testament Gospel and the coming of Jesus, and we have the biggest collection of miracles yet! And then on to the fourth era – that of Pentecost and the coming of Christ's Spirit – another surge of miracles.

Why do they take place? They occur as authenticating hall-marks of God's revealed truth as it comes to us in the Scriptures. Naturally that does not bar the occurrence of miracles at other times in history. After all, God is God! Indeed, we sometimes hear reports of miraculous healings from the distant frontier outposts of the faith in lands where Christianity has yet to get established. What is happening? Simply this: God is authenticating his messengers of the Gospel in virgin territory.

It is for this reason that the occurrence – or non-occurrence – of miracles is not in itself an accurate thermometer of spiritual temperature!

'If anyone believed that I could be healed of my paralysis, I did!' said Joni Eareckson Tada from her wheelchair. It was February 2000, and the world-travelled Christian leader and author was speaking with Paul Blackham, a colleague of mine, and myself. We were filming for the *Open Home, Open Bible* study programme.

'Following the diving accident at the age of seventeen, I read up everything on healing, and I was convinced that healing was mine for the claiming,' said Joni. 'I even rang my friends and said, "You'll be seeing me on my feet tomorrow!" Then when I wasn't healed, I decided that I needed to have a closer look at the Scriptures. Verses like John 14:12: *I tell you the truth, anyone who has faith in me will do what I have been doing. He will do even greater things than these, because I am going to the Father.*'

– 'And of course, no one has ever done greater deeds of physical healing than Jesus,' I chipped in – 'healing at a distance, feeding 5,000 people, the raising of Lazarus....'

– 'So it wasn't deeds of a superior quality, was it?' added Paul Blackham, 'but rather deeds....'

– 'Of a greater *dimension*,' finished Joni. 'It's the context of the Holy Spirit and his coming, in that passage, that gives the clue.

'There was the New Birth by the Spirit' ....

– 'And,' added Paul, 'When you think of it, those first Christians numbered only a very few people, when Jesus ascended. But then comes Pentecost, and suddenly thousands are added!'

– 'Together with the growing world-wide fellowship of believers, all connected simultaneously with Jesus by the Spirit,' said Joni, 'Such a thrilling thing can certainly be described as *greater works*!'

'You know,' she added, 'I travel all over the world. Of course there are miracles of healing here and there. But I've been able to see, with the passage of time, that actual miracles of physical healing are really very few.'

'Why don't we have water turning into wine any more?' demanded an agnostic of his Christian neighbour.

'Well, I don't know about water into wine,' replied the Christian, 'but I do know that today God can turn beer into furniture.'

'What?'

'Certainly. I used to be a hopeless alcoholic. I'd ruined the family. I'd sold most of the furniture to pay off my debts. Then Christ came into my life. My drink problem is a thing of the past now, and the house is furnished once again!'

I well remember a church member who was nearly killed in a terrible car smash some years ago. His life seemed to be hanging on a thread. There were literally hundreds of Christians who prayed for him. No miracles took place and yet, slowly, by infinitesimally painful degrees, the long crawl back to health began. A couple of years after the accident, Mike confided, 'At one point the question was raised as to why there shouldn't be a miracle healing in my life, and the whole thing be put right at a stroke. But as I thought about it, I rejected the idea. I realized that it was better this way. Over the months I've learnt so much from God, and I've grown as a Christian in a way that I couldn't have done if there'd been a sudden healing.'

Prayer in the name of Christ is the way to the Father's heart, but it is not an automatic *Open Sesame*. To quote John Stott, 'This is ridiculous. It would turn prayer into magic, man into a magician like Aladdin, and God into our servant like genii summoned to do our bidding whenever we rub our little prayer lamp.'

Christian prayer is very different from the workings of mediumism or magic, whether black or white. Where is the dividing line when it comes to the 'borderline' areas, to the strange healing movements which surround us today?

The difference is this. Once try to 'force' a result through your prayers, once 'use' prayer, or even the name of Christ, as a formula in your desire to obtain a certain result and you are teetering on the edge of mediumism, where *man* is in the driving seat and the power of God is seen as an energy to be harnessed. Christian prayer is quite, quite different. Here, we are in the area of *relationships*, where we, as trusting children, place a need or an individual decisively into the hands of the heavenly Father, *confidently leaving the result to him.*

It is of paramount importance that those of us who are believers live and breathe in the atmosphere of God-centeredness, of Gospel-centeredness. This will drive us to our knees in intercession, and incite us again and again to reform our lives, our churches, and, so far as we are able, our world, in line with the Word of God – Dr. Don Carson, *The Gagging of God* (Apollos).

16

POWERHOUSE

Terrifying? Initially perhaps. I can remember the first time I attempted to participate in a prayer gathering. I could hear my voice wobbling out of control. And where had my verb got to? It was only later that I came to realize that the grammar and choice of words are of minor importance on such occasions. Split infinitives and mixed metaphors are part of everyday speech, and so it is almost inevitable that they will occur when Christians pray together. 'O God,' prayed one man fervently in his prayer meeting, 'if there has been a spark of revival kindled in this gathering, then we pray that you will *water* that spark!'

Read the accounts of the early Church, and you will see that these Christians prayed together:

> *So Peter was kept in prison, but the church was earnestly praying to God for him (Acts 12:5).*

There's something about praying together. Certainly there was in this case, because the answer to this combined prayer was that Peter was released from prison, much to the surprise of the prayer group members! A girl's report that he was free, and standing outside the door of the prayer meeting, was met with flat disbelief. And they'd been praying for this very thing!

> *'You're out of your mind!' they told her. When she kept insisting that it was so, they said, 'It must be his angel' (Acts 12:15).*

Again and again it has been demonstrated that God delights to take action within his world, but it is also apparent that his chosen way of action is with the co-operation of his praying people. Jesus re-inforced this idea when he told his disciples, 'Whenever two of you on earth agree about anything you ask for, it will be done for you by my Father in heaven. For where two or three come together in my name, there am I with them' (Matt. 18:19, 20).

What a marvellous statement! Even the smallest possible congregation of Christ's disciples, that of two people, has an assurance of being *heard* when it unites in prayer! It is not that we have met together in a charmed circle, in a coalition that can somehow bend its influence upon God, forcing an answer from him. There is no magic in a prayer meeting. No, the very words of Christ here imply that we are meeting as *disciples* whose chief concern is, naturally, for the will of their master. And the very fact that a number of disciples can agree upon a joint topic of prayerful concern is in itself a strong indication that God's will has been clarified, more so than if one person prayed alone. The great joy of praying together lies in the fact of the Almighty God of the universe choosing to use our prayers and our co-operation to bring about his will in people and places altogether outside our control. I do not think, biblically, that our joint prayers affect God's will. But they do seem to affect his action!

Why then do we not pray more often together? Frequently a prayer group just does not exist, or if it does, it is the optional extra among the other meetings and is attended perhaps by the 'left-overs' who somehow don't fit in anywhere else! But praying together should, in reality, be seen as the powerhouse of all of God's work. Can we wonder at some of the reverses that come the way of the Christian cause if these important times are not taken seriously? Can we wonder why our services and meetings fail to become irradiated with life, if we do not pray about them?

Frequently we leaders are at fault. Church prayer meetings, as such, have tended to be side-lined – when they ought really to be at the centre! *On Prayer Meeting night, no other church activities ought to be taking place.* It needs to be understood across the board that anyone aspiring to be a leader or worker in the fellowship should be pledged to the regular, united prayer gathering. Before being appointed to any position, it is as well to ask the aspiring leader, 'Will you be a regular member of the prayer gathering?' Children's workers, youth leaders, Church Council members, house fellowship leaders, Sunday service welcomers, worship leaders – everybody who has taken on a piece of service in the church needs to block off the prayer meeting dates right through the year – together with other regular members.

Of course allowances should be made for such contingencies as family anniversaries, illness or the need for a husband and wife to split forces because of children at home. But church leaders do well to avoid taking outside Christian engagements on prayer meeting night – *because all too often prayer is the first thing to go.*

The prayer meeting has earned itself rather a dull profile across the years; long straight rows of chairs, long lists of obscure names and topics, long rambling intercessions, long silences, long faces! This has got to be reversed. Preparing a room for a prayer meeting is an acquired art. That rubbish in the corner has got to be dealt with, the chairs should be arranged in a way that suggests a natural family get-together. It's best not to bunch the chairs close together, but to space them out, yet if possible to give the impression that they are filling the room! Psychologically it is better to put out too few chairs than too many; no one likes to be looking at empty seats, and spirits will rise if the call goes out 'We need more chairs, please!' And how about a drop of coffee at some point – even some supper – and a little music as people come in?

The leader of the church gets up at the start; yes, generally it ought to be the leader – the minister – who is seen to be leading the church at prayer. A welcome, some opening words of worship, a song or hymn, and then into some topics for praise. A little coaching may be necessary:

– 'Let's try and keep these prayers short, so that others can have a turn!... Keep that little voice *up*, if you can, so that we can all hear you and come in with our *Amen*.... If you lead us in prayer keep your private prayers out of it. At that moment you are spokesperson to God on behalf of all of us!... Don't worry if silence falls! It's just as spiritual to pray silently, as it is to pray aloud'....

So this is public 'out-loud', extempore praying. It is caught as much as taught. It should not be too frightening, provided that the leader can set a style that is relaxed and cheerful, non-manipulative and non-spooky!

Praise follows, then a Bible 'focus' verse. Not a Bible study; just a verse, a story, a brief application – five minutes at most. And then intercession – for the church, its Sunday services, the preaching, the music, the welcoming, the newcomers, the children's activities, the money! Is there some special event being hosted by the fellowship? Let it be prayed for. If the Gospel has a hold on the prayer gathering, the prayers should follow, thick and fast. Beautiful phrases are not necessary. In one of the Billy Graham team meetings, one member, John Dillon, had spent the whole day at his desk, dictating letters. His prayer ended with these words:

And so Lord, we thank you for being with us today. Yours sincerely, John Dillon.

As we advance towards the events we have prayed about, a surge of confidence ought to take hold of the prayer meeting members – *we prayed about this*.

Another song, and then perhaps into the 'main' topic. Is it the turn of the students to be featured on this occasion? Let a couple of their leaders introduce the slot ... briefly! It is all too easy for an allotted three-minute slot to elongate into six, eight or even ten minutes; you'd be amazed. *It is actual prayer that is the first thing to go*. It frequently happens that leaders will fill up a prayer meeting with singalongs, notices, testimonies and over-detailed lists of names flashed up by the overhead projector – *we'll do anything but pray*!

Is there a point during the meeting when it is right to switch from the 'open' prayer format to the forming of small groups of not more than five or six in a group? This, for some, is a relief; for others it is even more terrifying! Crucial to the whole operation is the approach of the overall leader; there simply has *got* to be confidence that the prayer gathering is in reliable, trustworthy hands.

Sometimes this necessitates some gentle

firmness. I remember leading a prayer gathering at All Souls Church, into which had come a man of unbalanced and extreme views. During the prayers he suddenly spoke up:

– 'I am now able to announce to you that the next Archbishop of Canterbury is to be Richard Bewes....'

He got no further.

'No,' I interrupted. 'This gathering is for intercessory prayer, and for nothing else. Let me give out one or two more topics, and then we'll pick up again. Let's not forget to pray for' – and I mentioned some further needs. The prayers resumed.

Presently the same voice interrupted again.

– 'I have been in the counsels of the Lord, and I am now able to tell you that the Second Coming of Christ is going to take place at midnight on the....'

Before he could name the date, I cut in again over the top.

'I wonder whether Clive and Bill here would be so kind as to take our friend here outside the room, have a chat with him and find out what's on his mind?'

The three men went out, and we continued praying. It was not a massive hassle, but the lesson was there once more: *the first thing to go is actual prayer*.

How to close? Perhaps the prayer gathering can end with a sizeable World Mission chunk of time. In this way, the prayers will have followed an ever-outgoing pattern, finally fanning out to issues and people thousands of miles away. In this way the message steadily gets across – *Your church could touch the world.*

A final hymn, a closing prayer, and a few announcements ... *and did it end at the announced time*? Confidence to come back the next time will be built if the leader resists the calls of the prayer zealots to prolong matters. Bring the proceedings to a punctual halt – however ruthlessly!

So how is the corporate prayer life of the fellowship? The famous evangelist Gipsy Smith once said in a sermon, 'In the model church, the people will love to pray. They will love that more than anything else. They would rather go to a prayer meeting than to a place of entertainment. When the church of God uses the Apostolic standard, it will be a praying church. That will be its chief characteristic. *These people prayed.*'

We must leave them in the hands of God ... and to seek Christ alone as our comfort. All other roads are dangerous – Maurice Wood

17

THE DEPARTED

The barrier between life and death seems almost paper-thin shortly after the death of a loved one. Immediate contact has been lost – and we wonder wistfully whether it could not, in some way, be restored?

There is much to reassure Christians at this point. First, the only truly 'safe' Christian is a dead Christian! The pilgrimage is over, the battle is done, and the departed believer is with Christ. We owe it entirely to Christ that, for the worst enemy of all, we now use the best name, sleep! 'Our friend Lazarus has fallen asleep,' he said, 'but I am going there to wake him up' (John 11:11). He used the same term in the case of Jairus's daughter (Luke 8:52). How little his hearers understood him! After all, his own resurrection had not taken place at that stage. Things are different now, and we understand better: 'But Christ has indeed been raised from the dead, the firstfruits of those who have fallen asleep' (1 Cor. 15:20).

Bible students are divided over the question

of this 'sleep'. Are Christ's people, upon leaving this life, called into the immediate *conscious* presence of the Lord – such a state being called 'sleep' primarily from the point of view of the believers who are *left?* There is a convincing case for such a view (see Luke 9:30, Luke 16:19-31, Heb. 12:1). Or are these departed believers in an *unconscious* state – albeit in the direct care of Christ – awaiting the final day of full resurrection and reunion? (1 Thess. 4:13-18) Practically speaking, it makes no difference as far as the departed ones are concerned – their first *conscious* experience, after death, will be of Christ and his glory. But whatever the precise nature of this 'sleep', we are left in no doubt about our proper attitude to the departed.

When someone is asleep you take care not to disturb him! There are devout men and women of prayer who have, over the centuries, made the mistake of attempting communication with the world of the dead. They have sometimes addressed their prayers to the departed, in the hope that they will act in a kind of 'postman' capacity, and carry their prayers to God. This is pointless. Departed believers are not reachable; they are asleep in Christ for the time being. In any case, we can come to Christ direct with our petitions, because in him 'we have a great High Priest who has gone into the very presence of God' (Heb. 4:14 GNB). He is the only 'postman' for our prayers that we should ever want. Fully God and fully man, standing alone in his sinlessness, having dealt, through his death, with the sin barrier that would otherwise have blocked the way to our prayers, there is simply no one else who could qualify in getting us a hearing with God. For this reason, believers love to conclude their prayers with words like 'For Jesus Christ's sake', 'Through Christ our Lord'.

So we do not pray to those who have passed on. *Nor do we attempt to disturb them in any way.* There is, in fact, in the Bible, an absolute ban on all mediumistic activity, seances and the like:

> *But people will tell you to ask for messages from fortune tellers and mediums, who chirp and mutter. They will say, 'After all, people should ask for messages from the spirits and consult the dead on behalf of the living.'*
>
> *You are to answer them, 'Listen to what the Lord is teaching you! Don't listen to mediums – what they will tell you will do you no good' (Isa. 8:19, 20 GNB).*

If communication with the world of the dead has no place in the Christian's prayer life, what about prayers *for* the faithful departed? Is this a valid activity? Let us look at this positively.

I shall never forget the day early in 1977 when Janani Luwum, beloved Anglican Archbishop of Uganda died, while in the custody of the government militia. I had met him three years earlier in Lausanne at the great Evangelism Conference with Billy Graham. I had been greatly impressed with him. He had been prayed for regularly in our own church fellowship. And now he was dead. Every time I think of Janani, that shining light, my thoughts are turned into prayers – prayers of thankfulness for his courage and love, and for the wonderful example he left us all. What is significant is that my prayers have altered in their direction. I no longer pray *for* the departed believer as I used to when he was in the thick of the Christian fight, facing pressures and demands from all sides. He is out of all that now, asleep awaiting the day of resurrection and reunion (1 Thess. 4:16, 17). There is no point in praying that he may be kept *safe*. He is totally, eternally safe with Christ. To pray for his welfare now would be to express a lack of confidence in the Gospel promises:

He who sits on the throne will protect them
with his presence. Never again will they
hunger or thirst; neither sun nor any
scorching heat will burn them, because the
Lamb, who is in the centre of the throne, will
be their shepherd, and he will guide them to
springs of life-giving water. And God will
wipe away every tear from their eyes (Rev.
7:15-17).

So to fellow-believers who have lost a loved one, we must emphasize that it would clearly be difficult, if not impossible, to 'switch off' your prayers concerning someone for whom you have probably prayed for many years. That would not be right. *But learn to change the direction and content of your prayers now.* You no longer have direct touch with your loved ones – that is true. But you are in direct touch with *Christ,* who has them in his care and keeping. This tremendous factor will affect your prayers, and turn them into repeated expressions of thankfulness and confident trust.

Often our desire to maintain contact with the dead stems from a misunderstanding about the nature of our world and theirs. If we understood better something of the life that is in store for Christ's followers, as revealed to us in the Bible, we would not be nearly so eager to keep a hold on our departed friends. Do we *really* want them back with us?

There are those who say, 'Oh, if only people could be raised today, as Lazarus was in the Bible.' But think for a moment about that amazing event involving the dead Lazarus, in John 11. The dead man stumbles out of the tomb, raised to life again at the command of Christ. 'Untie him,' Jesus told them 'and let him go.'

Go? Go where? Why, back to the home in Bethany. It would be lunch time in a few minutes. It would be his turn on the washing up! And tomorrow would see Lazarus chatting with his neighbours once again, over the garden fence, in just the same old way! Off to the supermarket to do the shopping for Martha and Mary. He'd be doing his tax returns next. *He had been brought back to the old life again –* the old life, with its relationships, its responsibilities, its problems, its aches and pains. And one day Lazarus was going to die again, and go through the whole process once more!

So what was this miracle saying to us? This certainly – that Christ has the power to release people from the winding sheet of death. But this electrifying event with Lazarus was only an illustration, a foretaste of the real thing to come. There was, inevitably, a limitation in this miracle, wonderful as it was. It was only the curtain-raiser! When Jesus, in New Testament days, raised people from death, whom did they awake to see? Why, Christ the conqueror of death. They had been brought back into the world where *he* was, right here on earth. What would be the point of people being resurrected today if they were going to miss the encounter with Jesus in the next world?

We live today in an infinitely greater dimension than the one in which even Lazarus lived. For 'resurrection' today means a going *on* – to greater powers and greater glory. It means a pain-free life in a resurrection body in the immediate presence of the glorified Christ. It's living and reigning with him for ever! When Christ rose from the grave, it wasn't a coming *back*, a return, but a moving forward. So it will be with all who today are linked to Christ. Let us not feel too wistful about our departed fellow-believers, in the light of all this. Surely we don't *want* them connected once again with the old life, with its daily adversities and the gradual erosion of energy and powers.

Years ago, when large passenger ships were about to leave for another country, the scenes on the quay-side would become very emotional. A passenger on the liner would hold on to the end of a long paper streamer. The other end would be grasped by a friend on the quay, reluctantly bidding farewell to the traveller. Sometimes fifty or a hundred such streamers would be unwound, stretching over the widening strip of sea as the ship slowly moved out into the channel. The last connection between those departing and those left was about to be snapped. It would be preserved until the last moment. Paper-thin! And then it was gone.

We do not have to torture ourselves in this way. *Let them go*. We need have no fears for our loved ones in Christ. At present they are asleep in him, awaiting the day of awakening, when they will have resurrection bodies like his. Let us thank him for them, and for their security in his keeping power. And let's always remember that the day of reunion is getting closer, when, away from the aches and trials of the old life, we shall, with all Christ's family, be united, face to face. With him!

To him who is able
to keep you from falling
and to present you
before his glorious presence
without fault and with great joy –
to the only God our Saviour
be glory, majesty,
power and authority,
through Jesus Christ our Lord.
before all ages,
now and for evermore!
Amen.

(A doxology from Jude 24)

When I saw those men walking on the moon, and they were showing us the world by television, I wanted to reach out and grab it for God! – Billy Graham

18

AMBITIOUS PRAYER

Out in Kenya, when I was about six years old, I got a tennis ball at the bottom of my Christmas stocking. It was just about the loveliest thing I had ever held or smelt! Up to then any tennis ball I'd encountered had been muddy brown in colour, worn smooth by repeated contact with sun-baked courts, and with a mysterious rattle inside! This was different. White, fluffy and brand new, it was a prize object to be stored carefully away in a drawer. Certainly it was not to be *played* with. From time to time I'd bring it out and smell it again. Wonderful! Occasionally someone would say, 'Where's that tennis ball of yours? Let's have it out. Give you a game!' But I would shrink away in horror. 'No, no! Not today. It might get spoilt.'

However some three years later I did in fact bring it out for a game. Whatever had happened? There was no bounce left in it at all! In the tropical heat, the rubber had simply perished to nothing. Jesus once said something a little reminiscent of my experience:

*Whoever has something will be given more,
but whoever has nothing will have taken away
from him even the little he thinks he has (Luke
8:18 GNB).*

In the thinking of Jesus, to 'have' something implied more than mere passive possession. *Really* to have it necessitated constant use and application. Hearing and doing go together in the Christian life. *Having* is *using!* Thus the incident of my tennis ball is only an illustration of the parable of the talents, in which the man who did nothing with the one talent entrusted to his care lost it altogether. You either use it, or you lose it! So it is with all that we are given to use for the service of God.

Two people are reading the same newspaper. One exclaims with indignation at the atrocities being perpetrated in a certain totalitarian regime – and turns on to the holidays supplement in the centre. The other remains still, silently projecting mind and heart, in an unspoken prayer on behalf of the Christians and missionaries of that country. Which of the two individuals is exercising a greater influence upon the world?

'What a mystery prayer is!' wrote Max Warren 'I sometimes wonder if we do not make it more difficult by trying to rationalize it, reduce it to a method.... May not a visit be a prayer, a conversation a prayer, a letter a prayer... ? Deep down I do not believe that this is being lazy. I wonder if it may not point the way to something rather exciting. "He walked with God" – that might not, at first showing, be a definition of prayer. Is there a better one?' (*Crowded Canvas*, Hodder).

'The world is opened by prayer,' asserted Toyohiko Kagawa of Japan. If this is so, then more of us must learn, through prayer, to turn the events and news of daily life to good account. We may never have been out of our own country physically, but we can learn to make the prayer leap, over the barbed wire, across border controls, penetrating invisibly and silently into countries where our passports might gain us no access at all. It's no use trying to compass the whole world every time we pray. Better, perhaps, *to select target areas for our praying*, and to do this with a plan and a method. It's not enough to pray 'Bless, O God, all the Christian leaders in India.' Can we utter the name of a single Christian in India – a sub-continent with some billion people? If not, why not? The world is a global village, we are always being told. If the earth is so tightly wired, and we have all been brought closer to one another, how is it that a Christian could *not* know the names of some fellow-believers in Peru, Morocco or Indonesia?

I remember a worker from the Sudan telling me of his visit, while on leave in England, to the church with which he had been specifically linked for prayerful support. The Sudan had not been without a fair measure of tension and difficulty during the time he had served the Church there. The minister got up to introduce the 'Link Missionary'.

'Well, it's a great pleasure for me now to introduce Monty to you – and he's going to tell us all about the work that he's been doing over in – er ... out in ... um – *Abroad*!' This from the leader of the church that was supposedly 'praying' for him.

If vision and prayer for God's international family is very limited, then *begin humbly – but specifically*. Start with *one* name – preferably that of someone who has visited your fellowship or church. Have a photograph of the individual or of the family. See to it that news letters get to you with information that will help your praying to be relevant and sharp. Take the magazine of the Christian agency with which that individual may be linked. It's all very well to say blandly, 'Ah, but the whole world is now the mission field – we don't need to concern ourselves with organizations and societies.' As Stephen Neill once commented aptly, 'When everything is mission, *nothing* is mission.'

When we have learnt to pray for one person or cause beyond our own horizon, we should *add another*. We should make it the thrill of our lives to influence and touch, by our unseen prayers as much of this world as God will give us strength for – and to leave the earth a better place as a result. It should be the same with our Christian work and witness 'at home'. Which neighbour, friend, or associate are we praying for by name, with a view to their being won over to the faith we have in Christ? *Names*, which names?

Leaders in God's work should ask themselves, periodically, what targets are they prayerfully aiming to achieve in our work next year, that we are not achieving this year? Does our church have a house group in operation at present? That is very good! When, by God's grace do we hope to have two? So you're a visitor with the church newspaper? Delivering to no less than twenty houses in your road? Wonderful! When do you trust to be doing thirty?

You either use it, or you lose it! And

prayerful ambition is the key. 'Prayer,' said Alfred Stanway of Australia, 'will empty people's pockets much faster than speeches.' Either we believe Alf Stanway to be speaking the truth and we act accordingly, or we behave as the world has always done, when it comes to the raising of money – and join the frenetic circuit of vociferous appeals, giant red thermometers, bazaars, jumble sales and the whole shooting match. As a minister once said wonderingly, 'When I first arrived to take over the leadership, the church was riddled with whist!'

Start small, but start definitely. Write it down in a list if necessary:

the targets
the aims
the people

It's no use saying 'Ah, nothing's happening, the people around me have no vision.' It's your business – and mine – to create this vision. Prayerfully!

Here am I.
Send me!

*(A prayer of the prophet Isaiah,
Isaiah 6:8)*

When the storm passes over, the grass will stand up again – Kikuyu proverb

19

AN ALL-WEATHER FAITH

Two mice were once paddling in a bowl of milk. Round and round they swam. At last one of them got tired and said in desperation, 'It's no good going on any longer – I'm giving up!' With that, it sank beneath the milk and was drowned. But the other little mouse hung on gamely to the end. On and on it paddled, round and round until at length the milk turned to butter and it crawled out safe and sound!

The staying power of the Christian life is not discovered in a flash. It is built up a day at a time. And the time to be adding to the reservoir of prayer and experience is during the 'in between' periods, when nothing dramatic is happening and we are not swimming desperately for survival. We often think that those are the least significant phases of living. Those waiting periods – waiting for exam results, waiting for a prayer to be answered, waiting for the doctor's report, waiting for the promised job that has not materialized. But these are *the* significant times! Most of life is composed of the waiting times, and the difference between one Christian and another frequently lies in what is done with these 'in between' periods, when there is no crisis, and excitements are down to a minimum.

'We have no right to count on God in the agony of a crisis,' wrote F B Meyer, 'unless we have been walking in fellowship with him previously.' How hard it is to pray when things are dull!

Praying in the dull uneventful times is an indication that we are in earnest with God. Similarly when we pray in the face of delayed answers to our continued praying. Why is it that we are subjected to delays? A delay is frequently a test of our earnestness. Too often our requests are no more than casual *wishes* that flit vaguely across our thinking only to be totally forgotten an hour later. This seems to be the point of Christ's parable of the loaves at midnight (Luke 11:5-10). Bold and persistent praying gets what it seeks – always assuming a true basis of relationship and a genuine need. This is a story, not about the reluctance of God, but about the persistence of true prayers. Success comes from asking, even in our imperfect human relationships, and even in the face of a barred door, a sleeping householder and a flat refusal ('I can't get up and give you anything'). But God is utterly unlike the grudging householder in virtually every detail. 'Friend, let me borrow three loaves!' Yes, but is *God* a lender? He is supremely the great giver. God never answers 'from inside' (v.7). God never says 'Don't bother me!' *And to God it is never midnight.*

How much more then should we persevere in the requests we make to him! It is true that a prolonged delay may indicate that we are asking for the wrong thing, in which case it acts as a corrective to our praying. It is also possible that unconfessed sin is the cause of our inability to obtain an answer (Isa. 59:1, 2). But then think of the delay in answer to the plea from Martha and Mary that Jesus should come to the help of the sick Lazarus (John 11:3ff). Why did he take his time in honouring the request of two close and trusted friends? Was this not an instance of the principle once given in reply to a query about continuing evil – that often what we call evil is really 'unfinished good'? Martha and Mary could not see the 'resurrection' end of the story, and it was not surprising that they asked for a short-term benefit. There are times when we simply cannot see clearly with the eyes of faith, and must content ourselves with the prayer of limited objectives. 'Brave' prayers for the outright overnight conversion of a godless dictator can too easily be the glib thoughtless prayers of an immature faith. Someone else, a little further 'in' might pray, with a greater depth of faith and expectation, that the same dictator might receive a copy of the Scriptures.

Again and again, when aware of friends, colleagues and relations who seem to be spiritually unresponsive, the prayer can be *Make them hungry, Lord*. Try it. You will have those names on your prayer list. As you go through the names, bring each individual to God's throne – with the prayer, 'Make them hungry, Lord'.

Pastors do well to pray inside their churches on Saturday night, before the Sunday services. Go to the main front door, and commit to the Lord the men and women, girls and boys, who will be entering the building tomorrow. Ask that none may escape what God has to say to them. *Make them – make us all – hungry, Lord.* Place the whole building under God's protection. Pray firmly that no person, power or spirit may be allowed into the services tomorrow that do not have God's express permission. Walk around the church; between the rows of seats, and ask that the Holy Spirit will do his work in worshipper after worshipper who will be there tomorrow. Stand in the pulpit, and ask that *tomorrow* – at the very moment the preacher comes to this same pulpit, that the power of God may descend, and that over and beyond the words of the preacher, another voice will take over, and listeners may know that God himself is speaking! And as the message is delivered, *Make them hungry, Lord.*

We can do this anywhere in the world, whether we are worshipping in a great cathedral, a school hall or a prison.

Or, indeed, in a church that has been vandalised and left roofless. In a particularly unstable region of the world, during the course of a single violent night, 126 churches were burnt to the ground by religious extremists. This was in July, 1998. The Christians asked their leaders, 'What shall we do?'

– 'Do? Do nothing! Turn up for worship as usual on Sunday. Same time, same place!'

And they did, by the thousand. As they stood in the blackened ruins of their churches, they sang, prayed and listened to the preaching. It was an extremely powerful witness. But something else happened too. It was the time of the rains, when it was usual for the downpour to continue for weeks on end. In this case there was no exception – but for one thing. All around that region *it never rained on Sundays*. For eleven Sundays in a row the Christian worshippers were able to meet in their roofless buildings – without a drop of rain falling on them.

This phenomenon was not unobserved by the perpetrators of the attacks. First – there had been no revenge attacks. And then it appeared that the Christians' God was smiling on them with Sunday after Sunday of sunny weather! Here was a message that spoke volumes.

Do we find it difficult to believe, and to go on praying, in an exploding world, seemingly out of control? 'Your faith was born in violence,' declared a preacher from the Third World, in whose own country a coup had taken place.

'The Christian is not scared when Ghana is upset, when Indonesia is trembling, when the whole world is shaking. Your faith was born on Calvary – *it can stand anything*. It's an all-weather faith.' Come to Calvary itself, and we can feel the force of that remark. For is it not here that we have the greatest instance of a prayer that was not granted? 'My Father, if it is possible, take this cup of suffering from me! Yet not what I want, but what you want' (Matt. 26:39). The salvation of the world depended upon that prayer not being granted.

The world is like a vulnerable space-ship today, a space-ship with a limited supply of oxygen and with its own 'self-destruct' mechanism built in. 'Oh, if only we could find a hiding place!' wrote Alexander Solzhenitsyn in *Gulag Archipelago*.

What does the life of prayer achieve?

Men and women can do one of two things. They can allow themselves to be *in* the storms that rage around the planet, and yet remain mentally detached from them, unaffected by their terror. Or they can let the storms penetrate into the very living room of their souls and blow them where they will. Life with God in the secret place is the life that can stand back a little from the world, understand it and shape it.

'Until I became a Christian, I had no idea what the world was about; I simply couldn't understand it.' So said Donald English, one-time president of England's Methodist Conference. He added, "I can't feel at home in this world any more." I know what they mean, but *my* testimony is that I *do* feel at home in this world – at last!'

20

NOT REALLY THE LAST WORD

God, heavenly Father,
The story of my life is not unlike the writing of a book.

The dawning of each day is not unlike the turning of a fresh new page, white and clean, perfectly blank, waiting to be filled with the actions and words of today.

I am ashamed when I think of those earlier pages, of the volume of days that went to make up the story of my life.

It was your Son who made the difference to my record, by his entry into our world.

Living and dying, he wrote a new story, my story.

Father, let me dedicate this new day to you, in love and gratitude for all that you have done.

May I see today as the writing of a new fresh page, the story of my life in yours and yours in mine.

Richard Bewes